Creative Chain Mail Jewelry

Colorful • Sophisticated • Classic

KB
KALMBACH BOOKS

Kalmbach Books
21027 Crossroads Circle
Waukesha, Wisconsin 53186
www.Kalmbach.com/Books

Published in 2011
15 14 13 12 11   1 2 3 4 5

Manufactured in the United States of America

ISBN: 978-0-87116-421-6

Compiled by Erica Swanson
Art Direction: Lisa Bergman
Layout: Rebecca Markstein
Illustration: Kellie Jaeger
Photography: William Zuback, James Forbes

Publisher's Cataloging-in-Publication Data

Creative chain mail jewelry / [from the publisher of Bead&Button, BeadStyle, and
  Art Jewelry magazines].

   p. : col. ill. ; cm.

  "Colorful, sophisticated, classic."
  "29 beautiful projects from the pages of Art Jewelry and Bead&Button magazines."-
-p. [4] of cover.
   ISBN: 978-0-87116-421-6

   1. Chains (Jewelry)--Handbooks, manuals, etc. 2. Metal-work--Handbooks,
manuals, etc. 3. Beadwork--Handbooks, manuals, etc. 4. Jewelry making--
Handbooks, manuals, etc. I. Kalmbach Publishing Company. II. Title: Chain mail III.
Title: Bead&Button magazine. IV. Title: Art Jewelry magazine.

TT212 .C742 2011
745.594/2

Contents

Projects

Introduction

The art of chain mail has endured throughout the years. Beginning as armor, this unique wire-weaving technique has been perfected to make gorgeous, substantial jewelry. Whether you enjoy traditional sterling silver chains or are looking for different ways to incorporate chain mail techniques, you'll find the perfect match.

You can begin making your own chain mail jewelry with just a handful of jump rings and a pair of pliers. With projects pulled from the pages of *Art Jewelry* and *Bead&Button* magazines, this volume contains a little bit of everything. Build a timeless Byzantine chain, construct a sinuous, slinky Persian weave, or make a freeform necklace from jump rings. Once you've mastered the basics, you can add crystals, try your hand at additonal wirework techniques, or break out your jeweler's bench to do a little easy soldering. Whatever your skill or style, you'll find complete instructions for making a beautiful accessory.

Materials

Jump ring metals

Jump rings are available in a wide range of materials. Gold and silver are the most traditional choices, but you can find jump rings made from brass, copper, steel, and niobium, among other options.

Silver

There are four common options for silver: fine silver, sterling silver, Argentium silver, and German silver. Of these, fine silver is the purest, composed almost entirely of silver. However, fine silver is a fairly soft material, so it is not ideal for chain mail. If certain elements don't require a lot of strength, such as a head pin for hanging a single bead, use fine silver. It will stay white and lustrous without much polishing since it oxidizes at a slow rate. It also doesn't have to be pickled after heating if used without flux.

Sterling silver and Argentium silver are perfect for most jewelry-making applications, since they have been alloyed with other metals for additional strength. Sterling silver has long been the material of choice for jewelry makers, since it is strong and malleable. Sterling silver is 92.5% fine silver with 7.5% copper and other metals — thus the .925 stamp on sterling. The drawback to sterling is that this small copper content makes it oxidize at a faster rate than fine silver, so it tends to tarnish quickly. Argentium silver is an alloy that substitutes a higher content of germanium to avoid the tarnishing problem while retaining the strength of the metal. Argentium is considered a great technological advancement in silver, having the best qualities of sterling without its oxidation rate, but Argentium is a bit stiffer than sterling to work with.

German silver wire is frequently found in beading stores and craft shops. This wire is formed by layering sterling silver over a copper core. If you have exposed wire ends (as on wrapped loops), or if you need to hammer your wire, the copper core will show. For that reason, many jewelry makers avoid German silver wire.

Gold

Gold wire is available in different karat weights, tempers (see p. 6), and even colors. Pure, 24k gold is very soft to work with, while 14k gold is a 7/12-gold alloy. For those of you who love the warm, silken appearance of gold but want to keep the costs of your jewelry-making endeavors affordable, gold-filled jump rings are an economical choice. They're a fraction of the cost of 14k-gold wire. Contrary to its name, gold-filled wire is actually gold overlay. A thin layer of 24k gold is heat- and pressure-bonded to a brass core. The layer of pure gold makes the wire tarnish-resistant, and it should be cared for just like the expensive version. Gold-filled wire should be buffed with a soft, clean cloth (such as flannel) and stored in a dry place. Placing tissue paper around your gold-filled wire will minimize exposure to humidity and prevent scratching while it's being stored.

Niobium

Niobium has the same strength as half-hard sterling silver, but it's about 20 percent lighter. One of the great things about niobium is that it's hypoallergenic. Many people who can't wear silver or other common jewelry metals wear niobium with no negative effects.

Niobium gets its color from an anodizing process, which coats the surface of the metal with an oxide layer. This is accomplished with an electric charge. The voltage of the charge determines the thickness of the oxide layer, which in turn determines the color. Anodizing is used to prepare many metals for dyeing, because the porous oxide layer allows dye to enter. The same process turns titanium and niobium a range of colors without the use of dyes.

The colored surface of anodized niobium is just that — on the surface. The layer of color is easily scratched, exposing the natural silver color of the niobium.

Gauge

Wire gauge is the measure of a wire's thickness, or diameter. The higher the gauge number, the thinner the wire. Thicker wire is more difficult to work with, while thinner wire has less strength. Using the correct gauge is crucial for producing a chain mail weave, so follow the materials lists carefully.

Shape

The wire used to make jump rings also comes in a variety of shapes, ranging from the traditional round profile to half-round, flat or square, triangular, and twisted. You can make your own twisted wire by twisting two pieces together.

Temper

The temper of wire is its hardness, or malleability. Silver and gold wires can be purchased at different levels of hardness, such as dead-soft, half-hard, or full-hard. Working with wire strengthens it; this is called work-hardening. Jump rings for chain mail are most often half-hard.

Inner Diameter (ID) vs. Outer Diameter (OD)

When choosing jump rings, be sure to note whether the supplier is measuring the rings by their inner diameter (ID) — the size of the mandrel the jump ring is made on — or the outer diameter (OD).

WIRE GAUGE CHART			
American Gauge	British Gauge	Diameter (inches)	Diameter (mm)
10	12	0.102	2.6
12	14	0.081	2.1
14	16	0.064	1.6
16	18	0.051	1.3
18	20	0.040	1.0
20	22	0.032	0.8
22	24	0.025	0.6
24	26	0.020	0.5
26	28	0.016	0.4
28	30	0.013	0.32
30	32	0.010	0.26

PREVENT SCRATCHING

Some artists use tape (green florist's, masking, athletic, and blue painter's) to cover the jaws of the pliers in an effort to protect the jump rings, but tape adds heft to the pliers, which, for someone who's used to making chain mail, is like playing the piano while wearing gloves. Florist's tape doesn't stick, masking tape is too rigid, and athletic tape slides off. Blue painter's tape tears and leaves sticky blue specks on the jump rings that has to be removed. The best solution is just to be careful.

The most common damage to jump rings is from sliding or scraping the pliers over the surface. So, weave the jump rings with your fingers, and use the pliers only to close the jump rings. Hold the jump rings firmly, and close them as cleanly and smoothly as possible; opening and re-grasping is much more likely to cause scratches.

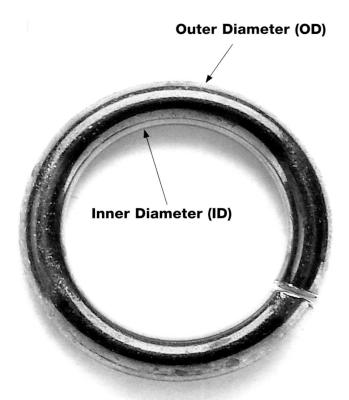

Outer Diameter (OD)

Inner Diameter (ID)

Tools

GAUGE

MILLIMETERS	22	20	18	16	14	12
2.0	●	●				
2.25	●	●				
2.5	●	●	●			
2.75	●	●	●			
3.0	●	●	●	●		
3.25		●	●	●		
3.5		●	●	●		
3.75		●	●	●		
4.0		●	●	●	●	
4.5		●	●	●	●	
5.0	●	●	●	●	●	●
5.5		●	●	●	●	●
6.0			●	●	●	●
6.5			●	●	●	●
7.0			●	●	●	●

• Ring sizes listed by inside diameter (ID) in millimeters.

• Rings shown closed to illustrate size more clearly.

• Wire gauges are standard AWG (American Wire Gauge) aka B&S (Brown & Sharp).

• Rings shown as close as possible to actual size.

If you love tools, there's no limit to what you can buy. The jewelry-making world keeps finding more and better ways to create beautiful pieces. The essentials that you absolutely have to have are pliers and cutters. We've included some of the more fundamental tools here, but when it comes to advanced tools, such as torches, it's best to do research and find the equipment that matches your budget and needs.

Pliers

Pliers are necessary for most wire-working tasks, including gripping and bending wire, and creating loops. There are also many specialty pliers, such as stone-setters, ring openers, and combinations that might be perfect for your needs. When purchasing pliers, inspect the jaws to see that they are smooth and even, look for a solid joint with a little give or wiggle, and try out the handle. When you spend a lot of time with tools in your hand, comfort is important. Here are some of the basic types of pliers and what they do.

Chainnose pliers have flat inner jaws, great for gripping jump rings and opening and closing loops.

Flatnose pliers are similar to chainnose pliers and can be used in the same manner, but have flat outer jaws, making it easier to make sharper bends in the wire.

Bentnose pliers are also close to chainnose pliers, but have a slight bend near the tips. Many jewelry makers prefer these pliers because they find them easier to use than straight chainnose.

Roundnose pliers are critical for making loops and bends. These pliers have conical jaws

Nylon-jaw pliers are another relative of chainnose pliers. These pliers feature replaceable nylon lining on the jaws, which protects wire from marks left by tools. You can achieve similar results by covering your pliers with tape or Tool Magic, but eventually wear and tear will affect the protection those aids offer. These are particularly useful with jump rings that have a thin coating of color that could easily scratch off, such as niobium.

Cutters

Side cutters are the most common type of cutters. As the name implies, these cutters have blades that are parallel to their handles. Some side cutters have blades that are tilted slightly upward. These are useful because they can cut wire from many angles. Side cutters produce a wide variety of cuts, each with their own strengths and weaknesses.

Flush cutters leave less of a bevel, and super-flush (aka ultra-flush) cutters are even better than flush cutters. They produce a flatter cut and require even less energy to use. However, in exchange for their tremendous cutting ability, super-flush cutters lose strength, so you can use them only for wire finer than 18-gauge.

Jeweler's saws have two components, an adjustable U-shaped frame with a handle, and a blade. You can use a variety of different blade sizes or thicknesses in the saw; use stronger blades for thicker metal. Saws are great for cutting shapes from metal and sawing through coils to make jump rings.

Dowels and mandrels

Dowels are circular rods, frequently made of wood, that jewelry makers use for shaping wire into jump rings and coils. Mandrels are made of steel, plastic, or wood, and have a smooth or stepped taper, so that rings and coils can be easily measured and removed.

Jewelry makers are frequently creative with their dowels and mandrels and often use other tools, like punches or knitting needles, as dowels and mandrels.

Torches

Torches are necessary for annealing and soldering wire components. They differ greatly in price range, temperature, and fuel. A wealth of material on torches is available, and those interested in using one should seek advice from trusted sources, such as online.

Files

Metal files are used to refine and shape the edges of metal and wire surfaces.

Jewelry-Making Techniques

Opening and closing a jump ring

1. Hold a jump ring with two pairs of chainnose pliers or with chainnose and bentnose pliers.
2. To open the jump ring, bring the tips of one pair of pliers toward you and push the tips of the other pair away.
3. The open jump ring.

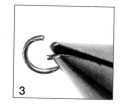
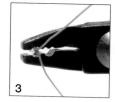

Making a folded crimp

1. Position the crimp bead in the hole of the crimping pliers that is closest to the handle. Holding the wires apart, squeeze the tool to compress the crimp bead, making sure one wire is on each side of the dent.
2. Place the crimp bead in the front hole of the tool, and position it so the dent is facing outward. Squeeze the tool to fold the crimp in half.
3. Tug on the wires to ensure that the crimp is secure.

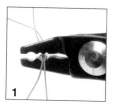
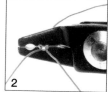

Making a plain loop

1. Using chainnose pliers, make a right-angle bend above the wire leaving an approximately ¼-in. (6mm) tail.
2. Grip the tip of the wire in roundnose pliers. Press downward slightly, and rotate the wire into a loop.
3. Let go, then grip the loop at the same place on the pliers, and keep turning to close the loop.
4. The closer to the tip of the roundnose pliers that you work, the smaller the loop will be.

Making a wrapped loop

1. Using chainnose pliers, make a right-angle bend above the bead, leaving an approximately 1¼-in. (3.2cm) tail.
2. Position the jaws of your roundnose pliers in the bend.
3. Curve the short end of the wire over the top jaw of the roundnose pliers.
4. Reposition the pliers so the lower jaw fits snugly in the loop. Curve the wire downward around the bottom jaw of the pliers. This is the first half of a wrapped loop.
5. To complete the wraps, grasp the top of the loop with chainnose pliers.
6. Wrap the wire around the stem two or three times. Trim the excess wire, and gently press the cut end close to the wraps with chainnose pliers.

Making jump rings

1. Select a dowel with a diameter that matches the inside diameter of the jump rings you want to make. Drill a hole through one end of the dowel, or saw a slot in the end of the dowel. Insert the end of the wire into the hole or slot to anchor it in place. Wrap the wire around the dowel, keeping the coils tight together [photo a].

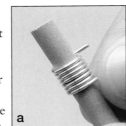

2. Cut the wire at the end that anchors the spring. Slide the spring to the opposite end of the dowel.

3. Secure the dowel against the V notch in your bench pin, and use a jeweler's saw to cut a shallow, vertical slot at the end of the dowel to guide your blade as you cut the spring [photo b].

4. Hold the spring and dowel with your nondominant hand. Saw through the top of the spring, feeding the spring toward the slot in the dowel. Be careful not to cut the jump rings in half, and be sure to have a catch tray or stretched apron below your bench pin to catch the falling rings as you cut them apart.

Tumble-polishing chains

The quickest, least labor-intensive way to make your sterling silver chains bright and sparkly is to tumble them with a fine porcelain medium in a vibratory tumbler. Small, tube-shaped porcelain bits with angled ends are available from most jewelry-making suppliers as "porcelain burnishing media." Using about 5 lbs. (2.3kg) of white/ultra-fine porcelain medium in combination with a burnishing liquid works wonders. You can also make your own burnishing liquid by mixing 1½ tablespoons (22.2mL) of powdered burnishing compound with 1 quart (.95L) of water.

1. Before you use your new porcelain tumbling medium, you must condition it. If you don't, it will leave a haze of fine scratches on your silver. Condition it by putting about 3½ lbs. (1.6kg) of new porcelain tumbling medium into a tumbler. Add a handful of large pieces of scrap silver. If you only have small bits of silver scrap or wire, melt them into larger blobs. These blobs will be easier to separate from the medium later, and they will condition the medium better than the tiny bits of wire.

2. Leave the tumbler uncovered, and plug it in. Slowly add burnishing liquid. Watch the action of the tumbler as the medium moves the metal pieces up along the outsides of the bowl and sucks them back down into the center. As you add liquid, this action will increase. When the action starts to

slow down again, you've added too much liquid. Unplug the tumbler, and pour some out. Screw the lid down firmly, and run the tumbler continuously for five days and nights. (Seven days is even better.) The liquid in the tumbler will become black and sludgy at the end of this conditioning period. Strain the sludgy liquid out of the tumbler into a bucket, and rinse the medium well. Combine the rinse water and the sludge, since the rinse water will also be black. If you love your drains, do not pour the bucket of sludge down them! Let the water evaporate, then put the dry sludge in a plastic bag and throw it away.

3. Clean the tumbler bowl, put the clean, conditioned medium back in the tumbler, and add a fresh serving of burnishing liquid (you do not need to change the burnishing liquid every time you use the tumbler). You are now ready to polish your chains.

4. You can also tumble patinated chains. If you have blackened your chains with liver of sulfur or another agent, try tumbling them overnight or longer. Depending on how long you leave the pieces in the tumbler, the chain rings will either emerge shiny black or display a dark-on-the-insides-but-light-on-the-outsides look.

Adding a liver of sulfur patina

Polish your piece before patinating. If you tumble-polish your piece after patinating, reserve the used shot for future patinated pieces; the liver of sulfur residue will contaminate other pieces.

1. Oil and dirt on the piece can affect the patina; use a degreasing soap to clean the metal before patinating.

2. Prepare a liver of sulfur solution according to the manufacturer's instructions. Using dedicated tongs, dip the metal in the solution for a few seconds, then rinse the metal in cool water to stop the chemical reaction. For a darker patina, continue to dip and rinse the metal. Use a brass brush with soapy water to remove or modify the patina. By using different temperatures and amounts of water to make the liver of sulfur solution, you can achieve different colors of patina; experiment to find the result you prefer. You can also apply liver of sulfur to selected areas of the metal with a small paintbrush.

Soldering

Solder is a metal alloy that is used to join two pieces of metal. You can buy solder as wire, paste, or sheet. Solder is available in different grades, ranging from extra hard to extra easy. The harder the solder, the slower it melts. For that reason, if there is more than one solder join in a piece, solder the first one using hard solder, the second using medium solder, and the third using easy solder.

Flux is available as a liquid powder or paste, and is used to coat a surface before solder is applied. Flux helps prevent oxides from forming on the metal when it is heated, which helps solder flow properly.

A torch is used to heat the solder and the pieces you wish to join.

Always use a fire-resistant surface, like a fire brick or charcoal block, and work in a well-ventilated area.

Water is used for quenching and rinsing the pieces. Fill two heat-resistant bowls: one to quench the piece after soldering, and the other to rinse off the pickle.

A solder pick is an awl-like tool with a metal tip and an insulated handle (such as wood) used to move and pick up solder while soldering. Solder doesn't stick to the metals used in solder picks, like steel, titanium, and tungsten carbide.

Pickle cleans the metal and dissolves the flux after the piece is fired. It is slightly acidic, so use it in a well-ventilated area, and take care to keep it off clothes, skin, and other surfaces.

Use copper tongs with pickle, as stainless steel will cause a copper plating of other metals in the pickle.

A warming pot can be used to keep pickle at a warmer temperature, which makes it work more quickly.

Prepare the join

All metal surfaces must be clean in order for solder to flow. Clean metal by sanding it with 400-grit sandpaper and rinsing it. The surfaces must be in complete contact with each other in order for the solder to join them — solder will not fill holes or gaps.

Flux and heat

Flux the area to be soldered to prevent oxidation. You can apply flux with a dropper or paint it on with a brush. Place the solder on the join and heat the entire piece, not just the solder. Keep the torch moving in a circular motion. Solder will flow toward the source of the heat, so once the solder begins to flow you can use your torch to direct it where you want it to go. When the solder flows, you'll see a flash of silver and it will move into the join. When this happens, immediately remove the heat.

Pickle and rinse

Once the solder flows, quench the piece in water, and place it in a pickle solution to remove oxidation and flux residue until it is clean and white (for silver). Rinse the piece in clean water.

Annealing

The temper of wire is its hardness, or malleability. Silver and gold wires can be purchased at different levels of hardness, such as dead-soft, half-hard, or full-hard. When working with metal, you want it to be pliable enough to manipulate, yet strong enough to hold its shape. Working with wire strengthens it; this is called work-hardening. Additional strength comes with hammering after you've formed your shape. The trick is to use wire that is soft enough to work with but becomes hard enough to hold the final shape. You likely will want to work with half-hard wire the majority of the time. When connecting elements with double-wrapped loops, the act of wrapping the loops is enough manipulation to fully work-harden the wire so it is at its maximum strength. If you used full-hard wire, it could be too difficult to manipulate. If you use dead-soft wire, it could only become half-hard after wrapping, so it would not maintain its shape as well. Most projects in this book will specify which temper works best for each project.

Annealing is the process of heating work-hardened metal until it softens enough to be malleable. Put your metal on a fire-resistant surface, and heat the metal with a torch until it glows a subtle pink. Immediately remove the heat when you see the color, or you'll burn or melt the metal. Dim or turn off the lights to help you see this color change. To finish, quench the metal in water and put it in warm pickle to remove any oxides.

Projects

Knot
bracelet

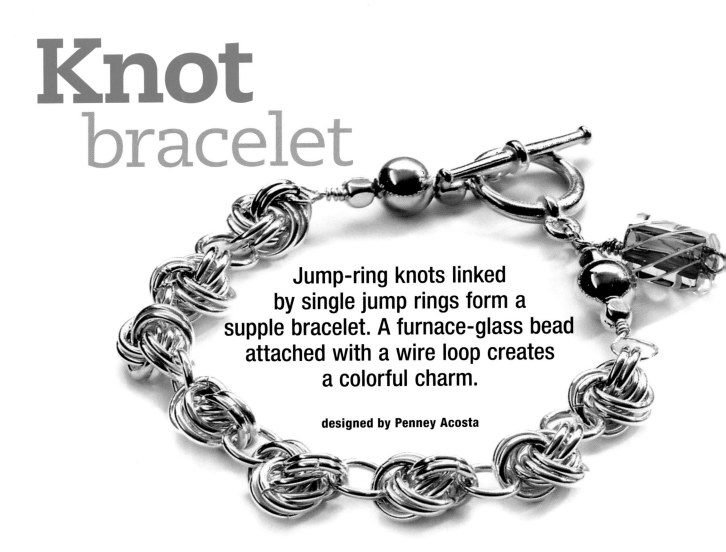

Jump-ring knots linked by single jump rings form a supple bracelet. A furnace-glass bead attached with a wire loop creates a colorful charm.

designed by Penney Acosta

MATERIALS

bracelet, 7 in. (18cm)
- **71** sterling silver or gold-filled jump rings, 5.5mm ID, 16-gauge
- 10–15mm furnace-glass bead
- **2** 6mm silver or gold-filled accent beads
- **4** 3mm silver or gold-filled accent beads
- clasp
- 12 in. (30cm) 22-gauge sterling silver or gold-filled wire, half-hard
- bentnose pliers
- chainnose pliers
- roundnose pliers
- wire cutters

Jump ring knots

► **1** Close two jump rings and open six jump rings.

► **2** Slide the two closed jump rings on an open jump ring [photo a]. Close the jump ring.

► **3** Slide an open jump ring on the pair of jump rings [photo b]. Close the jump ring. Place the cluster on a work surface and position it as shown [photo c].

► **4** Slide a jump ring through the center hole of the cluster [photo d]. Close the jump ring.

► **5** Repeat step 4 and position the two jump rings just added as a pair.

► **6** Slide a jump ring through the center hole of the cluster. Do not split the pairs of jump rings. Close the jump ring [photo e].

► **7** Repeat step 6 to add the last jump ring.

► **8** Repeat steps 1–7 seven times to make a total of eight jump ring knots.

Assembly

► **1** Open a jump ring. Slide it through one pair of jump rings on each of two knots [photo f]. Close the jump ring.

a

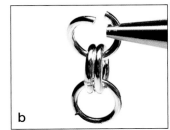

b

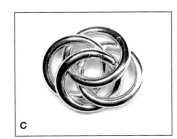

c

d

e

f

► **2** Open a jump ring, and slide it through the pair of jump rings opposite the connector jump ring just added **[photo g]** and a pair of jump rings on the next knot. Close the jump ring.

► **3** Repeat steps 1 and 2 to connect all the jump ring knots. Do not attach a second connector jump ring to the last knot.

► **4** Cut three 4-in. (10cm) pieces of 22-gauge wire.

► **5** On one wire, make a loop at one end. String the furnace-glass bead, and make the first half of a wrapped loop.

► **6** On one of the other wires, make the first half of a wrapped loop large

enough to accommodate two jump rings. On the loop, string the pair of jump rings opposite the last jump ring connector. Finish the wraps. String a 3mm accent bead, a 6mm accent bead, and a 3mm on the wire. Make the first half of a wrapped loop, attach half of the clasp, and finish the wraps. Trim the excess wire.

► **7** Repeat step 6 on the other end of the bracelet, making the second wrapped loop large enough to accommodate the clasp and the loop of the charm. Attach the charm to the second wrapped loop and finish the wraps.

PROJECT NOTE:
If you're using a thin furnace-glass bead like the one in the gold bracelet, string the wire through the hole and make a set of wraps and a loop above it.

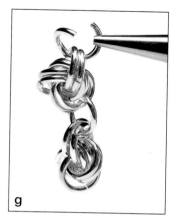

g

Bicycle chain
bracelet

Adding glass rings to easy chain mail creates a lively, colorful bracelet. For casual elegance, try gemstones or matte glass in a single color.

designed by Luan Carnevale

PROJECT NOTES:

- Glass rings offer regularly sized holes, but 10mm gemstone donuts also work well for this project. Make sure the holes in the gemstones are large enough to loosely fit four jump rings. You may need to increase your jump ring size to 6.4mm or 7mm to fit around two donuts and four jump rings.
- If silver is too precious for your pocket-book, get started with an easy-to-use base metal like aluminum, or add some color with anodized aluminum jump rings.
- If you have leftover glass rings, try making a matching necklace. Follow steps 1–4 of the bracelet, and then link pairs of rings to each end until the necklace is the desired length.

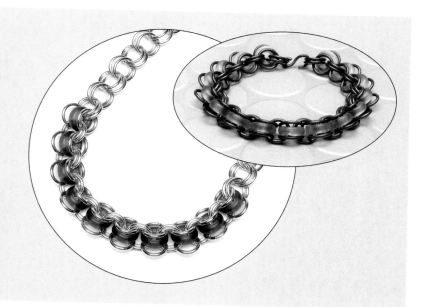

a

b

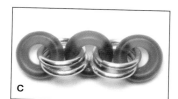
c

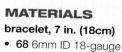

d

e

f

g

h

i

MATERIALS

bracelet, 7 in. (18cm)

- **68** 6mm ID 18-gauge jump rings
- **16** 9mm glass rings, cheerios, or donuts with 4mm hole
- fold-over clasp
- **2** pairs of chainnose pliers

Bracelet

▶ **1** Open a jump ring, attach two glass rings, and close the jump ring [photo a]. Open a second jump ring, slide it through the same two glass rings to sit parallel to the first jump ring, and close the jump ring [photo b].

▶ **2** Open a jump ring, attach a new glass ring to the previous glass ring, and close the jump ring. Repeat with a second jump ring [photo c].

▶ **3** Open a jump ring. Position the four jump rings attached to the second-to-last glass ring near each other, and attach the new jump ring to the four jump rings above the glass ring. Close the jump ring [photo d]. Flip the chain over and repeat on the other side, so the glass ring is sandwiched between two jump rings [photo e].

▶ **4** Repeat step 2 [photo f] and step 3 [photo g], and continue building the chain until the bracelet is 1 in. (2.5cm) short of the desired length.

▶ **5** Attach a pair of jump rings to the glass rings at each end of the bracelet, and then repeat step 3 at each end [photo h].

▶ **6** Open a jump ring, and attach the clasp and the two jump rings at one end of the bracelet. Close the jump ring [photo i]. Attach a jump ring to the two rings at the other end of the bracelet.

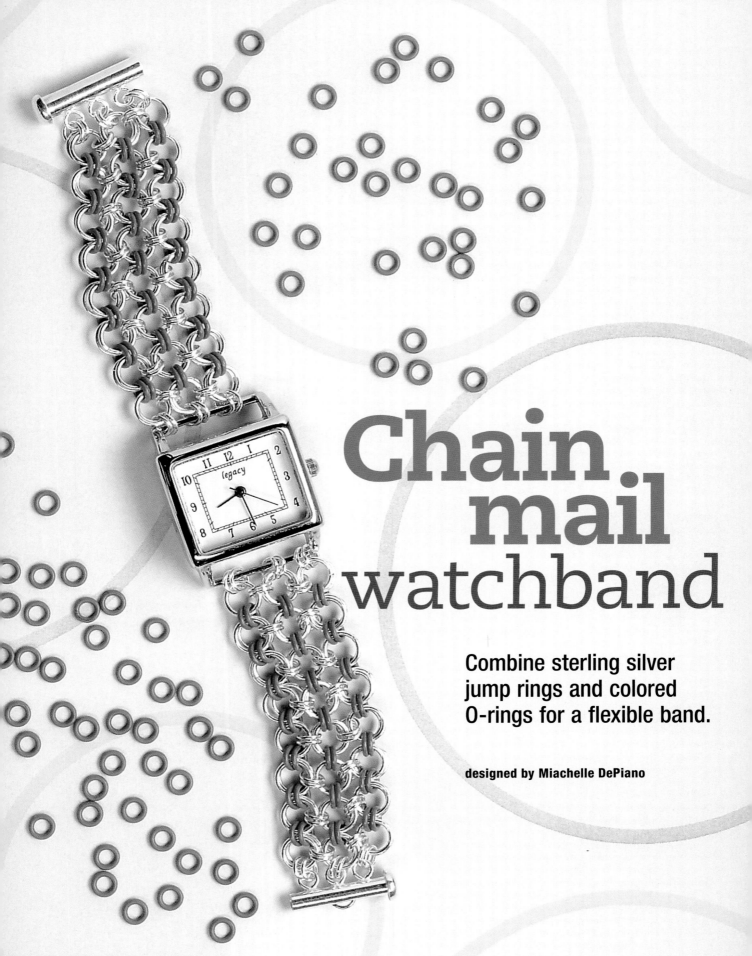

Chain
mail
watchband

**Combine sterling silver
jump rings and colored
O-rings for a flexible band.**

designed by Miachelle DePiano

MATERIALS

watch, 6 in. (15cm)

- ribbon watch face 1½ x 1 in. (3.8 x 2.5cm) (size can vary)
- slide clasp (bar or 3-strand)
- **84** sterling silver jump rings, 6.9mm OD, 19-gauge, **A**
- **80** sterling silver jump rings, 4.5mm OD, 21-gauge, **B**
- **72** rubber O-rings, 4.8–5mm
- bentnose pliers
- chainnose pliers

a

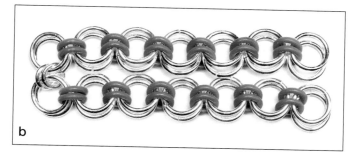

b

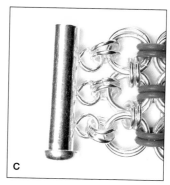

c

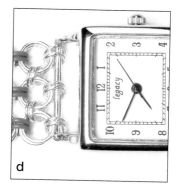

d

Watchband

▶ **1** Open 42 6.9mm A jump rings and 40 4.5mm B jump rings. Construct a 2+2 chain, which is a simple sequence of pairs of As and O-rings, using 14 As and 12 O-rings [photo a]. Repeat to make a total of three chains.

▶ **2** To attach two chains, slide two Bs around the first two pairs of As in each chain [photo b]. Repeat for the length of the chain.

▶ **3** Repeat step 2 to attach the third chain to the first two chains.

▶ **4** Repeat steps 1–3 to make a second watchband panel.

▶ **5** To attach a panel to half of a clasp, slide two Bs around each end pair of As and the corresponding clasp loop [photo c]. Repeat to attach the other end of the panel to the bar of a watch face [photo d].

▶ **6** Repeat step 5 for the other panel.

PROJECT NOTE:

To adjust the length of the watchband, add or omit three sets of jump rings per panel. This will increase or decrease the total length of the band by approximately ½ in. (1.3cm).

Rings
of color

Use niobium jump rings to add flashes of color to a traditional box chain. Alternate deep-purple jump rings with indigo jump rings in a repeating pattern, or feel free to experiment with more than two colors. Or, instead of a set color pattern, create a variegated effect by combining the jump rings in a random color scheme.

designed by Hazel L. Wheaton

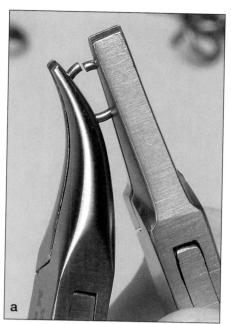

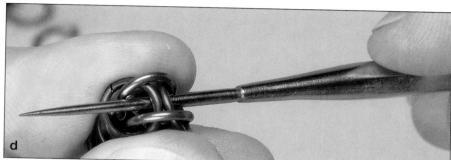

MATERIALS

bracelet, 7-in. (18cm)

- niobium jump rings
  - approximately **150** 18-gauge, 5mm ID
  - **6** 20-gauge, 5mm OD
- titanium clasp
- bentnose pliers
- chainnose pliers
- paper clip
- awl or needle tool

PROJECT NOTE:

As one can easily presume from another common name for this pattern, "idiot's delight," the box chain is an accessible pattern to master. Although it's slinky and appealing on its own, the box chain is also the foundation for other chain mail designs. For example, a simple variation on this chain creates the well-known Byzantine chain.

▶ **1** Hold bentnose pliers in your nondominant hand and chainnose pliers in your dominant hand. Grasp a jump ring firmly with both pliers, holding as much of the ring as possible in the pliers [photo a]; if you grip the jump ring at only one point, you're more likely to twist it out of alignment. Keeping the bentnose pliers stationary, rotate the chainnose pliers away from you to open the jump ring. Repeat to open a quantity of jump rings that will provide you with a ready supply for weaving the chain.

▶ **2** Set two unopened jump rings aside to use as starter rings.

▶ **3** Purchased jump rings are slightly open, so you will need to close the starter rings. Grasp one starter ring with both pliers in the same manner as in the previous step. Rotate your dominant hand inward, closing the jump ring. Repeat with the second starter ring.

▶ **4** Moving one half of the jump ring back and forth past the closure point work-hardens the metal and strengthens the finished piece. But the more you work the metal, the greater the possibility of scratching it, so work the jump ring no more than necessary.

▶ **5** Thread a paper clip through both starter rings to ensure that you work in only one direction. Thread an opened jump ring through both starter rings, and close it. Repeat with another jump ring. Thread a new jump ring through the second two jump rings, and close it. Repeat with another jump ring [photo b].

▶ **6** Push the third pair of jump rings apart to expose the second pair [photo c]. Push the second pair apart, and use an awl or needle tool to expose the third pair [photo d]. Thread a new jump ring through the third pair [photo e], and close it. Repeat with a second jump ring [photo f].

PROJECT NOTE:
The colored surface of anodized wire will not hold up to forging, so making your own colored clasp is not an option. If you want a clasp to match the colors in your bracelet, your best bet is to buy a colored clasp from a jewelry supplier. (The featured bracelet's clasp is anodized titanium.) Another option is to either buy or make your own sterling silver clasp and integrate jump rings into your chain pattern to match.

The chain pattern here is a 2+2 chain composed of anodized 20-gauge niobium jump rings and 18-gauge sterling silver jump rings. A sterling silver clasp completes the bracelet.

MATERIALS
• 20-gauge 8mm OD niobium jump rings
• 18-gauge 6mm OD sterling silver jump rings
• sterling silver clasp

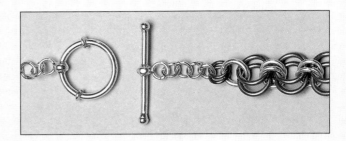

► **7** Thread a new jump ring through the fourth pair of jump rings, and close it. Repeat with a second jump ring [photo g].

► **8** Push the fifth pair of jump rings apart to expose the fourth pair. Thread a new jump ring through the fourth pair, and close it. Repeat with a second jump ring [photo h].

► **9** Continue adding extender rings and weaving until your chain is the desired length.

► **10** Remove the paper clip from the chain. Working with 20-gauge jump rings, attach two jump rings to the starter rings. To the two new jump rings, add one jump ring and the clasp. Repeat on the other end of the chain, omitting the clasp [photo i].

All the hoopla

Linked jump rings create a flat chain, allowing gemstones to fan out for maximum display. Use large jump rings for a bold statement or smaller jump rings for a more delicate version.

designed by Kimberly Berlin

MATERIALS

both necklaces

- bench block or anvil
- chasing hammer
- small file or wire rounder
- ruler
- chainnose pliers
- roundnose pliers
- flatnose pliers
- flush wire cutters

gemstone necklace, 17 in. (43cm)

- 5 15–20mm gemstone beads
- 4 8–12mm gemstone beads
- 5 4–6mm gemstone beads
- 18 4mm spacers
- 39 in. (.99m) 16-gauge round sterling silver wire
- 9 2½-in. (6.4cm) 22-gauge head pins
- 26 12mm ID jump rings, 16-gauge
- 21 6mm ID jump rings, 16-gauge
- 18 5mm ID jump rings, 16-gauge

crystal necklace, 17 in.

- 38 10mm ID jump rings, 16-gauge
- 53 4mm ID jump rings, 16-gauge
- 3 8mm round crystals
- 4 6mm round crystals
- 14 3mm faceted silver beads
- 7 4mm spacers
- 65 in. (1.7m) 16-gauge round sterling silver wire
- 7 2-in. (5cm) 22-gauge head pins

Note:

Some of the step-by-step photos show colored jump rings to make it easier to see the order of attachment.

Gemstone necklace

Links

▶ **1** Cut a 2½-in. (6.4cm) piece of 16-gauge wire. File the ends or use a rounder to smooth the ends.

▶ **2** Use roundnose pliers to turn a simple loop at one end of the wire. Make a simple loop on the other end of the wire as a mirror image of the first simple loop.

▶ **3** Using roundnose pliers, bend the wire in half with the backs of the simple loops touching to form a link [photo a]. Hammer the link. If the wire spreads, push the link back into shape.

▶ **4** Repeat steps 1–3 11 times to make a total of 12 links.

Clasp

▶ **1** Cut a 5-in. (13 cm) piece of 16-gauge wire, and file or round the ends.

▶ **2** Use roundnose pliers to make a plain loop at one end of the wire. Bend the wire into a hook so the simple loop almost touches the straight edge of the working wire [photo b]. On the other end of the wire, make a wrapped loop.

▶ **3** Hammer the hook and loop of the clasp [photo c].

▶ **4** Cut a 4-in. (10cm) piece of 16-gauge wire, and file or round the ends. Make a plain loop on one end, and make a wrapped loop on the other end. Twist the loops so they are perpendicular to each other, and hammer the loops [photo d].

Jump ring chain

▶ **1** Close 26 12mm jump rings, and open eight 6mm jump rings.

▶ **2** On a 6mm jump ring, attach two 12mm jump rings, and lay one to the left and one to the right of the 6mm jump ring [photo e].

▶ **3** Lay a 12mm jump ring over the 6mm jump ring [photo f].

▶ **4** Attach two 12mm jump rings as in step 2, and close the 6mm jump ring [photo g].

▶ **5** Flip the top right 12mm jump ring to the left. With an open 6mm jump ring, attach the bottom right 12mm jump ring and a new 12mm jump ring. Lay a 12mm jump ring over the 6mm jump ring as in step 3 [photo h].

▶ **6** With the open 6mm jump ring, attach the top right 12mm jump ring that was flipped in step 5 and a new 12mm jump ring. Close the 6mm jump ring [photo i].

▶ **7** Repeat steps 5 and 6 six times to attach all 26 12mm jump rings.

a

b

c

d

PROJECT NOTE:
Spiral components can add a new twist to the necklace.

e

f

g

h

i

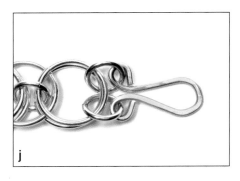

j

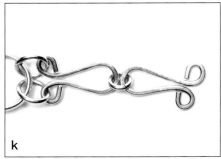

k

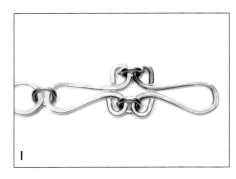

l

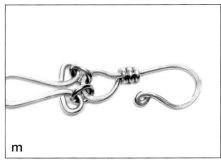

m

n

o

Necklace assembly

▶ **1** Open a 6mm jump ring, attach two end 12mm jump rings and a loop of a link, and close the 6mm jump ring. Repeat for the other loop of the link [photo j].

▶ **2** Open a 5mm jump ring, attach the center of the link and the center of a new link, and close the 5mm jump ring [photo k].

▶ **3** Open a 5mm jump ring, attach a loop of the link and a loop of a new link, and close the 5mm jump ring. Repeat for the remaining loops on the links [photo l].

▶ **4** Repeat steps 2 and 3 twice, but in the last repeat of step 3, attach half of the clasp instead of a new link [photo m].

▶ **5** Repeat steps 1–4 for the other half of the necklace.

Gemstone dangles

▶ **1** On a head pin, string a 4mm spacer, a 15–20mm gemstone bead, a 4–6mm gemstone bead, and a 4mm spacer. Make a wrapped loop to form a large gemstone dangle. Repeat four times to make a total of five large gemstone dangles, and set them aside.

▶ **2** On a head pin, string a 4mm spacer, an 8–12mm gemstone bead, and a 4mm spacer, and make a wrapped loop. Repeat three times to make a total of four small gemstone dangles, and set them aside.

▶ **3** Determine the order in which you want to attach the gemstone dangles. Open a 6mm jump ring, attach a gemstone dangle and a pair of 12mm jump rings, and close the 6mm jump ring [photo n].

▶ **4** Repeat step 3 for the remaining gemstone dangles.

Crystal necklace

▶ **1** Follow the steps in "Gemstone necklace: Links" to make 16 links using 2-in. (5cm) pieces of 16-gauge wire.

▶ **2** Make a clasp as in "Gemstone necklace: Clasp."

▶ **3** Make a jump ring chain as in "Gemstone necklace: Jump ring chain," but use 10mm jump rings in place of the 12mm jump rings and 4mm jump rings in place of the 6mm jump rings, and continue until you have connected all 38 10mm jump rings.

▶ **4** Connect the links and clasp as in "Gemstone necklace: Necklace assembly," but connect eight links on each side of the necklace.

▶ **5** To make a spiral dangle, cut a 4-in. (10cm) piece of 16-gauge wire, and make a small simple loop at one end. Repeat on the opposite end, making the loop face in the opposite direction [photo o]. Use roundnose pliers and your fingers to form a spiral with one loop until the spiral touches the other loop. Hammer the spiral.

▶ **6** Repeat step 5 five times to make a total of six spirals.

▶ **7** On a head pin, string a 3mm faceted silver bead, an 8mm round crystal, a 4mm spacer, and a 3mm. Make a wrapped loop. Repeat twice to make three 8mm crystal dangles, and four times with 6mm round crystals instead of 8mms.

▶ **8** Determine the order in which you want to attach the spirals and crystal dangles. Open a 4mm jump ring, attach a spiral or crystal dangle and a pair of 10mm jump rings, and close the 4mm jump ring.

▶ **9** Repeat step 8 for the remaining spirals and crystal dangles.

Link it up

Create a chain mail flower with
a clever series of jump ring
links. Aspect ratio plays a
key role in this bracelet.

designed by Wendy Hunt

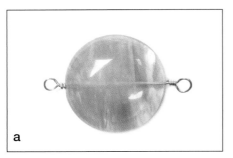

a

b

c

d

e

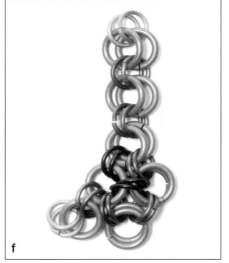

f

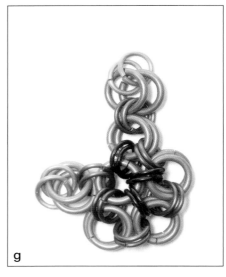

g

Bead components

▶ **1** Cut a 3-in. (7.6cm) piece of 21-gauge wire. Make a wrapped loop on one end. String an 18–20mm lentil bead, and make a wrapped loop [photo a]. Repeat to make a total of three lentil-bead components.

▶ **2** Cut a 3-in. (7.6cm) piece of 21-gauge wire, and make a wrapped loop on one end. String an 8mm bead, and make a wrapped loop. Repeat to make a total of four 8mm bead components.

Flower components

▶ **1** Open 24 2mm jump rings, and close 14 5.2mm jump rings.

▶ **2** On an open 2mm, attach four closed 5.2mms, and close it. Slide

another open 2mm through the four closed 5.2mms, and close it. This creates a 2+2+2 chain [photo b].

▶ **3** Slide an open 2mm through an end pair of 5.2mms, attach two more 5.2mms, and close it. Slide another open 2mm through the four closed 5.2mms, and close it [photo c].

▶ **4** Repeat step 3 to make a chain that has seven pairs of 5.2mms connected with six pairs of 2mms.

▶ **5** Slide an open 2mm through an end pair of 5.2mms, and close it. Slide another open 2mm through the end pair of 5.2mms, and close it. Repeat on the other end [photo d].

▶ **6** Slide an open 2mm through the second and fourth pairs of 5.2mms,

and close it. Repeat with a second 2mm [photo e].

▶ **7** Slide an open 2mm through the second and fifth pairs of 5.2mms, and close it. Repeat with a second 2mm [photo f].

▶ **8** Slide an open 2mm through the second and sixth pairs of 5.2mms, and close it. Repeat with a second 2mm [photo g].

▶ **9** Slide an open 2mm through the second and seventh pairs of 5.2mms, and close it. Repeat with a second 2mm [photo h].

▶ **10** Attach the end 2mms of the first and seventh pairs to the adjacent pairs of 5.2mms to complete the flower [photo i].

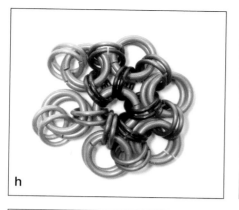

h

i

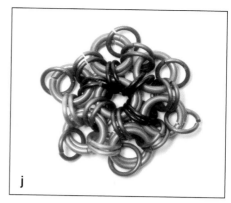

j

k

MATERIALS

bracelet, 8½ in. (21.6cm)

- 3 18–20mm lentil beads (jasper)
- 4 8mm beads (jasper)
- lobster claw clasp
- 21 in. (53cm) 21-gauge sterling silver wire, half-hard
- sterling silver jump rings
  - **9** 6mm (ID) 18-gauge
  - **84** 5.2mm ID 19-gauge
  - **18** 2.4mm ID 20-gauge
  - **180–216** 2mm ID 19-gauge
- chainnose pliers
- roundnose pliers
- wire cutters

l

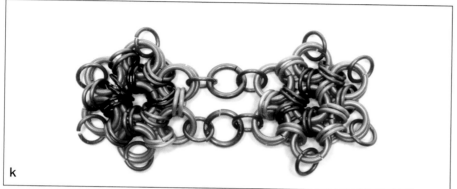

m

► **11** Open a 2mm, and attach it to an outer pair of 5.2mms, and close it. Repeat around the flower [photo j]. If desired, attach a second 2mm to each pair of 5.2mms.

► **12** Repeat steps 1–11 to make a total of six flower components.

Assembly

► **1** Open a 2.4mm jump ring, and slide it through the 2mm or pair of 2mms attached in step 11 of "Flower components" for each of two flower components. Repeat [photo k].

► **2** Place a lentil between the two flower components, and attach the remaining 2mms with 2.4mms as in step 1 [photo l].

► **3** Repeat steps 1 and 2 with the remaining flower components and lentils.

► **4** Open a 6mm jump ring, slide it through a wrapped loop of an 8mm and a lentil, and close the 6mm [photo m]. Repeat to connect the remaining 8mms and lentils, alternating between them.

► **5** Open a 6mm, slide it through an end wrapped loop of an 8mm, and close it. Repeat on the other end.

► **6** Open a 6mm, slide it through an end 6mm and the lobster claw clasp, and close it. Use the 6mm on the other end as the other half of the clasp.

Circular
chain mail
earrings

Combine colored metal and brass or sterling silver jump rings to make a pair of chain mail earrings. Colored jump rings make it easy to see the interlocking pattern.

designed by Sandy Amazeen

a

b

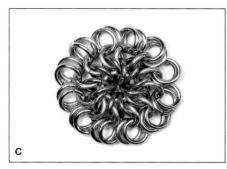

c

d

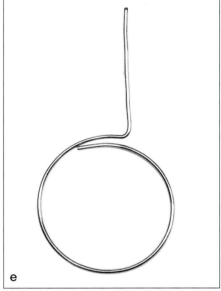

e

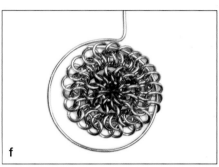

f

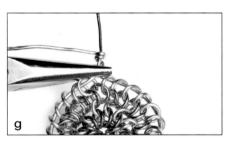

g

► **1** Open an 18-gauge 3mm brass jump ring and close 10 20-gauge 3mm color A jump rings.

► **2** Slide ten As on the 18-gauge jump ring. Close the 18-gauge jump ring. Open two more As, and attach them to the 18-gauge jump ring. Close the As [photo a], making sure they do not go through any of the previous As.

► **3** Open 12 20-gauge brass jump rings. Slide one open jump ring through two As and close the jump ring. Continue around the As, sliding a brass jump ring through the next A and in front of the second A of the previous pair. Connect the last brass jump ring through the back of the first A of the first pair and the front of the second A of the previous pair [photo b].

► **4** Open 24 20-gauge 3mm color B jump rings, and slide two Bs through each brass jump ring [photo c].

► **5** Open 24 20-gauge brass jump rings and connect one brass jump ring to a pair of Bs as in step 3 [photo d]

► **6** Cut a 6-in. (15cm) piece of 20-gauge brass wire. Bend the wire around a 1-in. (2.5cm) dowel. Make a right-angle bend on the top of the circle, leaving a ½-in. (1.3cm) overlap. Straighten the wire above the bend [photo e]. Put the wire frame on a steel block or anvil, and tap it with a hammer to harden it.

► **7** Slide the entire outer round of jump rings onto the wire frame [photo f].

► **8** To maintain the frame's diameter, grasp the crossed wires with chainnose pliers, and wrap the short tail around the long tail twice, making the wraps next to the pliers [photo g]. Trim the short wire.

► **9** String an accent bead and make a wrapped loop. Open the loop of an earring finding and attach it to the wrapped loop.

► **10** Make a second earring to match the first.

MATERIALS
earrings
- **2** 3mm accent beads
- 12 in. (30cm) 20-gauge brass wire
- **2** 18-gauge brass or sterling silver jump rings, 3mm ID
- 20-gauge brass jump rings, 3mm ID
  - **24** color A
  - **48** color B
  - **72** brass or sterling silver
- pair of earring findings
- 1-in. (2.5cm) dowel
- hammer
- steel block or anvil
- bentnose pliers
- chainnose pliers
- roundnose pliers
- wire cutters

Crystal
constellations

Be the center of your own universe! Make this freeform necklace featuring jump rings that orbit brilliant crystals.

Designed by Miachelle DePiano

a

b

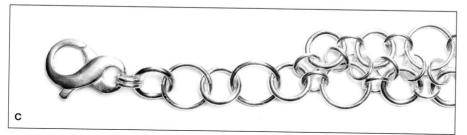

c

MATERIALS

necklace, 16 in. (41cm)
- jump rings
  - **5** 9.5mm ID, 14-gauge (A)
  - **62** 7mm ID, 18-gauge (B)
  - **60** 5mm ID, 16-gauge (C)
  - **131** 3.5mm ID, 20-gauge (D)
- bicone or round crystals
  - **5** 8mm
  - **4** 4mm
- lobster claw clasp
- **9** 2-in. (5 cm) eye pins
- straight pins (optional)
- 2 pairs chainnose pliers
- roundnose pliers
- wire cutters

Supply note:
Based on your personal design, quantities and sizes may vary.

Center design

▶ **1** Close all 9.5mm (A), 7mm (B), and 5mm (C) jump rings. Open all 3.5mm (D) jump rings.

▶ **2** Enlarge the template (figure) to 250 percent, go to BeadAndButton. com/resourceguide for a full-size template, or create your own template.

▶ **3** Attach your template to a flat surface, and arrange the A, B, and C jump rings on it to form the center of your design. If desired, use straight pins to keep the jump rings in place as you arrange them. Determine where you want to place the 4mm crystals, also.

▶ **4** On an eye pin, string an 8mm crystal, and make a plain loop. Repeat to make a total of five 8mm crystal units.

▶ **5** Open an A jump ring. Slide one loop of an 8mm crystal unit onto the jump ring, then slide the other loop onto the jump ring **[photo a]**. Close the jump ring, and place it back on the template. Repeat with the rest of the 8mm crystal units and A jump rings.

▶ **6** On an eye pin, string a 4mm crystal. Make a plain loop. Repeat to make a total of four 4mm crystal units.

▶ **7** Open a B jump ring. Slide the loops of a 4mm crystal unit onto the

jump ring as in step 6. Close the jump ring, and place it back on the template. Repeat with the rest of the 4mm units.

▶ **8** Starting at an outer edge of the center design, begin connecting the A, B, and C jump rings using the D jump rings **[photo b]**. Hold the chain mail section up frequently to check the drape. You may need to add, remove, or replace jump rings to adjust the shape.

Neck chain

▶ **1** On one side of the center design, begin attaching the B and C jump rings randomly to make the neck chain. This chain is two jump rings wide. Continue attaching jump rings until this half of the chain is the desired length minus the clasp.

▶ **2** Taper the chain to a single row of jump rings. Connect four or five B and C jump rings randomly. Use one or two Ds to attach the clasp to the end jump ring **[photo c]**.

▶ **3** On the other side of the center design, repeat steps 1 and 2, but in step 2 connect five to seven B and C jump rings and omit the clasp.

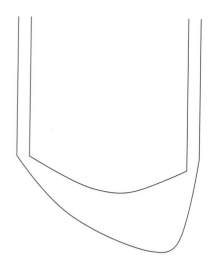

FIGURE

Tie the knot

Large jump rings lie parallel in this elegant wedding knot chain design. The drape of the finished piece, which is created by the weight of the silver rings, delivers the unmistakable feel of quality.

designed by Deanna Kittrell

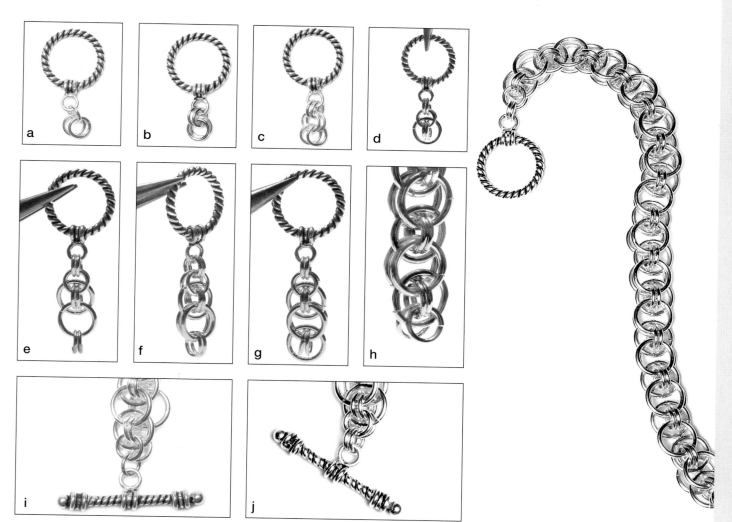

► **1** Open 46 7mm jump rings, open four and close 32 4.5mm jump rings, and open four 4mm jump rings.

► **2** Slide an open 4mm jump ring through half of a clasp and two closed 4.5mm jump rings. Close the 4mm jump ring [photo a]. Repeat to add a second 4mm jump ring next to the first [photo b].

► **3** Slide an open 4.5mm jump ring through the previous two 4.5mm jump rings. Close the jump ring. Repeat with a second 4.5mm jump ring [photo c].

► **4** Slide an open 7mm jump ring between the first two 4.5mm jump rings, surrounding the second two 4.5mm jump rings. Close the jump ring [photo d]. The 7mm jump ring does not go through any jump rings; it is held in place between jump rings.

► **5** Slide an open 7mm jump ring through two closed 4.5mm jump rings and through the last two 4.5mm jump rings. Close the 7mm jump ring [photo e]. Turn the chain over and add a second 7mm jump ring next to the one just added [photo f], enclosing the previous 7mm jump ring between the two new 7mm jump rings.

► **6** Slide an open 7mm jump ring between the two previous 7mm jump rings, surrounding the last two 4.5mm jump rings. Close the jump ring [photo g]. The 7mm jump ring just added, like in step 4, does not go through any jump rings.

► **7** Repeat steps 5 and 6 until you use all 46 7mm jump rings.

► **8** Slide an open 4.5mm jump ring through the last two 4.5mm jump rings, and close the jump ring. Repeat with a second 4.5mm jump ring on the other side of the 7mm jump ring [photo h].

► **9** Slide an open 4mm jump ring through the last two 4.5mm jump rings and the other half of the clasp. Close the jump ring [photo i]. Repeat with a second 4mm jump ring [photo j].

MATERIALS

bracelet, 8 in. (20cm)
- jump rings
  - **46** 7mm ID, 16-gauge
  - **36** 4.5mm ID, 18-gauge
  - **4** 4mm ID, 18-gauge
- clasp
- 2 pairs of bentnose or chainnose pliers

PROJECT NOTE:

To make a pair of earrings, work steps 2–4 and steps 8 and 9, substituting a single 4mm jump ring on each end in place of the clasp. Attach an earring finding to one end and a head-pin dangle to the other.

Dahlia
ring

Link jump rings in graduated
sizes to create a dimensional
ring. Use anodized aluminum
rings to create distinctive,
lightweight jewelry, and have
fun experimenting with
cheerful colors!

designed by Amanda Shero Granstrom

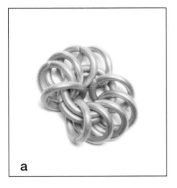

a

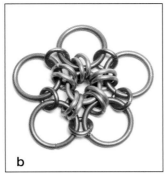

b

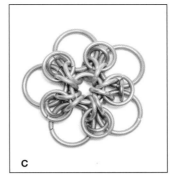

c

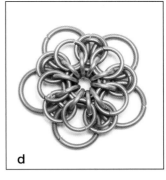

d

e

f

g

Flower

▶ **1** Close 10 color B 5mm jump rings, and open two color B 6mm jump rings. On an open 6mm jump ring, attach the 10 closed 5mms, and close it. Slide another open 6 mm through the 10 closed 5mms, and close it **[photo a]**.

▶ **2** Open five color A 10mm jump rings. Slide an open 10mm jump ring through two adjacent 5mms, and close it. Repeat to attach the remaining 10mms.

▶ **3** Open five color A 4mm jump rings. Slide an open 4mm jump ring through two adjacent 10mms, and close it. Repeat to attach the remaining 4mms **[photo b]**.

▶ **4** Decide which side of the flower is the front and which is the back, and build the next three layers on the front:

Layer 1: Open five color A 6mm jump rings. Slide an open 6mm jump ring through a color B 5mm in one pair and a color B 5mm in an adjacent pair, and close it. Repeat to attach the remaining 6mms **[photo c]**.

Layer 2: Open five color A 6mm jump rings. Slide an open 6mm jump ring through a pair of color B 5mms connected in the base layer in step 2, and close it. Repeat to attach the remaining 6mms **[photo d]**.

Layer 3: Open five color B 5mms. Slide an open 5mm jump ring through a pair of color B 5mms connected in the base layer in step 2, and close it. Repeat to attach the remaining color B 5mms **[photo e]**.

▶ **5.** Open five color A 6mm jump rings. On the back of the flower, slide an open 6mm jump ring through two adjacent 4mms, and close it. Repeat to attach the remaining 6mms **[photo f]**.

Ring

▶ **1** Cut a 7–10-in. (18–25cm) piece of 18-gauge wire. Make a free-form wire ball at one end by using chainnose and roundnose pliers to loosely wrap the wire into a small sphere big enough to prevent the wire from slipping through the hole in the center of the chain mail flower.

▶ **2** String the flower onto the wire with the wire ball on the front of the flower. Bend the wire on the back at a right angle. Wrap the wire twice around the mandrel for your desired size, keeping the wire ball tight against the flower.

▶ **3** Wrap the tail of the wire around the wire at the back of the flower, and trim **[photo g]**. File the end of the wire if desired.

MATERIALS

ring, 1¼ in. (3.2cm) diameter

- 7–10 in. (18–25cm) 18-gauge wire
- 5 10mm (ID) 16-gauge jump rings, color A
- 6mm (¼ in.) ID 18-gauge jump rings
  - **15** color A
  - **2** color B
- **15** 5mm ID 18-gauge jump rings, color B
- **5** 4mm ID 18-gauge jump rings, color A
- metal file (optional)
- ring mandrel
- 2 pairs of chainnose pliers
- roundnose pliers
- wire cutters

PROJECT NOTE:

To make sure you use the right amount of wire, string the flower onto the spool before making the ball. Make the ball, then measure 7–8 in. (18–20cm) of wire, and cut it from the spool.

Nestle
jump rings
between
crystals

Feminize a core of easy chain
mail with sparkling crystals.

designed by Deanna Kittrell

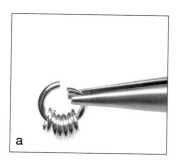

a

b

c

d

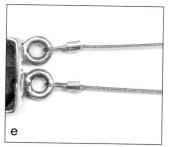

e

f

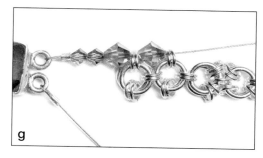

g

Bracelet

▶ **1** Close all the 3mm jump rings and open all the 5mm jump rings.

▶ **2** Slide six 3mm jump rings on a 5mm jump ring [photo a]. Close the 5mm jump ring.

▶ **3** Repeat the path with a second 5mm jump ring. Close the 5mm jump ring [photo b].

▶ **4** Pick up a 5mm jump ring, go through the two center 3mm jump rings from the previous step, and pick up six 3mm jump rings. Close the 5mm jump ring [photo c].

▶ **5** Repeat the path with a second 5mm jump ring [photo d].

▶ **6** Repeat steps 4 and 5 until you have 20 pairs of 5mm jump rings. To add the last pair of 5mm jump rings, pick up only four 3mm jump rings in step 4.

▶ **7** Cut two 12-in. (30cm) pieces of beading wire. On each end, string a crimp bead and the corresponding loop of half of the clasp. Go back through the crimp beads. Crimp the crimp beads, and trim the tails [photo e].

▶ **8** On one wire, string one or two 4mm crystals, a color A 6mm crystal, and the first two 3mm jump rings along one edge of the chain [photo f].

▶ **9** String a color A 6mm crystal (or a color B 6mm crystal if using two colors), and the next two 3mm jump rings [photo g].

▶ **10** Continue adding 6mm crystals (alternating color A and B crystals if using two colors) until you reach the last two 3mm jump rings. String a 6mm crystal, one or two 4mm crystals, and a crimp bead. Secure the end of the wire with tape.

▶ **11** On the second wire, repeat steps 8 and 9, but don't secure the end with tape. Remove the tape from the first wire. String the wires through the corresponding loops of the other half of the clasp. Go back through the crimp beads, but don't crimp them yet.

▶ **12** Close the clasp, and check the tension. There should be space between the crystals so the chain does not bunch up when it's worn. Crimp the crimp beads, and trim the tails.

MATERIALS
bracelet 7½ in. (19.1cm)
- **44** 6mm bicone crystals or **22** each of 2 colors: A, B
- **4–8** 4mm bicone crystals
- 1g size 15º Japanese seed beads (optional)
- 2-strand clasp
- **42** 5mm ID 16-gauge jump rings
- **124** 3mm ID 20-gauge jump rings
- **4** crimp beads
- flexible beading wire, .014
- bentnose pliers
- chainnose pliers
- crimping pliers
- wire cutters

Color
division

Make the move from flat to tubular chain mail with one additional step. Gravity and tension shape this necklace, holding the jump rings in a tubular configuration. Construct a two-colored flat European 4-in-1 band, then link the edges into a tube. Anodized aluminum jump rings create a lightweight necklace.

designed by Miachelle DePiano

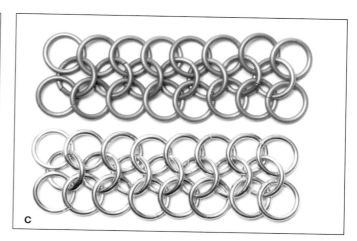

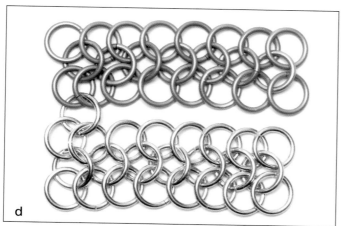

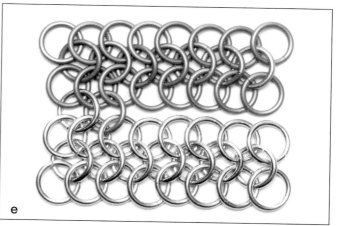

a

b

c

d

e

Necklace

▶ **1** Open 108 and close 104 color A 6.4mm jump rings.

▶ **2** Attach four closed A jump rings to an open A jump ring. Close the jump ring [photo a]. Set the 4-in-1 jump ring segment aside. Repeat 25 times.

▶ **3** To connect two jump ring segments, slide an open A jump ring through four adjacent jump rings in the two segments. Close the jump ring [photo b — note the placement of the purple jump ring]. Repeat with the remaining A jump ring segments to form a chain, linking each segment to the previously linked segments.

▶ **4** Repeat steps 1–3 with color B jump rings.

▶ **5** Place the A and B jump ring chains side by side [photo c].

▶ **6** To connect the chains, slide an open A jump ring through four adjacent jump rings. Close the jump ring [photo d]. The jump rings added in this step should have the same alignment as the purple jump ring shown in photo b. Repeat for the length of the chains, alternating an A jump ring with a B jump ring [photo e].

MATERIALS

necklace, 17½ in. (44.5cm)

- jump rings
  - **212** 6.4mm ID, 18-gauge anodized aluminum in each of 2 colors: A, B
  - **2** 3mm ID, 20-gauge sterling silver clasp
- **2** pairs of chainnose pliers
- ½ x 8-in. (1.3 x 20cm) strip of paper
- **2** toothpicks

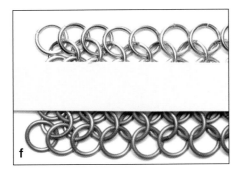

► **7** Flip the completed chain mail band, and straighten it. This will position the jump rings correctly to form the tube.

► **8** Place the ½ x 8-in. (1.3 x 20cm) strip of paper on the chain mail band **[photo f]**. Fold each edge of the band over the paper strip. Slide a toothpick through five or six edge jump rings to stabilize them **[photo g]**.

► **9** Slide an open B jump ring through four adjacent edge jump rings. Close the jump ring **[photo h]**. Slide an open A jump ring through the next unattached edge jump ring, the next two adjacent edge jump rings attached in the previous connection, and the next unattached jump ring. Close the jump ring **[photo i]**. Repeat for the length of the band, following the alternating color sequence. After you attach five or six connecting jump rings, remove the paper strip. Slide two toothpicks through the four end jump rings, and pull gently to form a tube. You will be able to see where the next

connecting jump ring needs to be placed **[photo j]**.

► **10** On one end, slide an open B jump ring through an end A and B jump ring. Close the jump ring **[photo k]**. Repeat with a second open B jump ring.

► **11** Slide an open B jump ring through the pair of B jump rings attached in step 10. Close the jump ring **[photo l]**.

► **12** Repeat steps 10 and 11 on the other end using open A jump rings.

► **13** Open a 3mm jump ring, and attach a single end jump ring and half of the clasp. Close the jump ring **[photo m]**. Repeat on the other end.

PROJECT NOTES:
• To increase or decrease the length of the necklace, add or omit a 4-in-1 jump ring cluster at the end of each color A and B chain. This will adjust the length by approximately ½ in. (1.3cm). Six jump rings are needed for each additional jump ring cluster.
• Vary the color of the connecting jump rings in steps 6 and 9 for interest. For example, alternate an A jump ring with three B jump rings.

Graduating
with honors

MATERIALS

necklace, 16 in. (41cm)
- sterling silver jump rings
  - **28** 7mm ID, 14-gauge
  - **28** 6.5mm ID, 14-gauge
  - **32** 6.5mm ID, 16-gauge
  - **32** 6mm ID, 16-gauge
  - **24** 5.5mm ID, 16-gauge
  - **32** 5.5mm ID, 18-gauge
  - **40** 5mm ID, 18-gauge
  - **12** 4.5mm ID, 18-gauge
  - **3** 4mm ID, 18-gauge
  - **48** 4mm ID, 20-gauge
  - approximately **48** 4mm ID, 20-gauge (optional)
- clasp
- chainnose pliers
- narrow flatnose or bentnose pliers
- 8mm, 7.5mm, 7mm, 6.5mm, 6mm, 5.5mm, 5mm, and 4.5mm wooden dowels (optional) flex shaft, drill bit (optional)
- bench pin (optional)
- jeweler's saw, 2/0 blades (optional)
- jump ring maker (optional)

Materials note:
A continual challenge in making a graduated chain is keeping the various types of jump rings organized. Count out the precise number of each size of jump ring you'll need, and clearly label each group of jump rings. Small plastic cups conveniently hold the jump rings, and the cups are easy to label with a permanent marker. Open each group of jump rings as you're ready to use them.

A simple rope pattern has long been a staple of jewelry makers for good reason: An elegantly twisted chain complements the pendant it shows off without overpowering it. Give the rope twist a graduated design, however, and you'll promote the chain from a supporting player to a lead performer capable of holding its own in the spotlight.

designed by Esther Lee

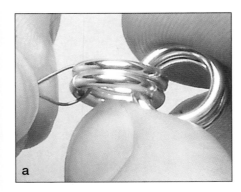

► **1** See the materials list to find out what jump rings you need. Either make the jump rings or buy them. Start with the 7mm ID 14-gauge rings. Jump rings come slightly open, so you need to close the starter rings. Hold your chainnose pliers in your dominant hand and your flatnose pliers in your other hand. Close the two starter rings, and open the other 26 rings.

► **2** Thread an open jump ring through the two starter rings, and close it. Repeat with a second open jump ring. To distinguish the end of your chain, thread a twist-tie or a piece of colored craft wire through the starter rings and twist [photo a]. Hold the linked rings so that the inside diameter of the second pair of jump rings faces you [photo b]. Thread an open ring through the hole in the center of the two pairs of linked rings [photo c], and then close the new ring. Repeat with a second open jump ring.

► **3** Hold the linked rings so that the inside diameter of the third pair faces you. Thread an open jump ring through the hole between the second and third pairs of rings, and close the new ring. Repeat with a second open jump ring [photo d].

► **4** Continue to add jump rings in pairs until you have added all the 7mm rings. Always make sure that the inside diameter of the last two rings you added faces you when you add the new rings; this makes it easy for you to see the hole through which to thread the next set of rings.

► **5** Open the 6.5mm ID 14-gauge jump rings, and separate them into two sets of 14 jump rings each. Add seven pairs of rings to the working end of your chain. Remove the twist-tie from the other end of the chain, and add the remaining seven pairs of rings [photo e].

► **6** Continue to add jump rings, opening a group of jump rings and separating them into two equal sets.

PROJECT NOTE:
The featured necklace, when finished, will be approximately 16 in. (41cm) long. To make the necklace more versatile, make an extender chain and add it to the back of the necklace when you want extra length.

► **1** Use 4mm ID 20-gauge jump rings to make your extender chain, following the same rope-twist pattern as in the project steps. Add jump rings until your extender is 2–3 in. (5.1–7.6cm) long; then add a clasp.

► **2** The extender is easy to clasp onto your necklace, and you can use it on other necklaces as well. You can make several extenders in various sizes, if you want more options.

Working in pairs, add one set of rings to each end of the chain. Then open the next group of jump rings and repeat until you've added all the rings and created a smoothly graduated chain.

► **7** If you want a longer necklace, add extra rings at each end of the necklace to maintain the balance of the necklace's center and the smoothness of the graduation. To keep your options open, make a simple extender chain (see Project Note).

► **8** When you have reached the desired length, attach a clasp. You can either make your own or purchase a premade clasp. Open the last set of jump rings on one end of the chain, link them through the clasp, and close the rings. Open the 4mm ID 18-gauge jump rings, and attach them to the other end of the chain.

Onward & upward

The interior portion of a Japanese overlay pattern links basic 2+2+2 chains to form the ladder-hybrid chain. Combine these two basic chains to form a new hybrid pattern.

designed by Anne E. Mitchell

Spend any amount of time looking at chain patterns, and you'll find that some of the most intriguing are made of two or more chain styles. These are called "hybrid patterns." The following hybrid is two standard European 2+2+2 chains linked by the interior portion of a Japanese overlay pattern.

The simplicity of this chain makes it a great one to start with on your chain-making journey. Use a magnetic slide clasp to finish the chain, and you'll have a beautiful bracelet or choker in a matter of hours.

Bracelet

► **1** Using the small, 5mm ID jump rings, make a 2+2+2 chain, which is a simple sequence of pairs of jump rings.

Make the chain as long as you want your bracelet to be; the featured bracelet is 22 link pairs long. Make a second 2+2+2 chain the same length as the first. Lay the chains next to each other [photo a].

► **2** Use liver of sulfur according to the manufacturer's instructions to darken the large, 7.5mm ID jump rings. Open the large jump rings, and lay one down between the two 2+2+2 chains [photo b].

► **3** Start at the left end of the top chain. Insert the large jump ring through the lower ring of the first link pair, then between the two rings of the second link pair, and out through the lower ring of the third link pair. Rotate the large jump ring another 90 degrees.

MATERIALS
bracelet, 7½ in. (19.1cm)
- sterling silver jump rings
  - **92** 5mm ID, 16-gauge
  - **11** 7.5mm ID, 16-gauge
- two-strand magnetic slide clasp
- bentnose pliers
- chainnose pliers
- padded work surface
- liver of sulfur

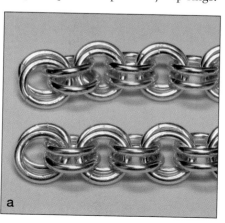

a

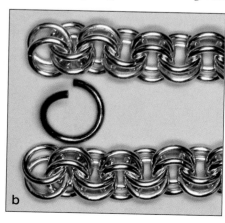

b

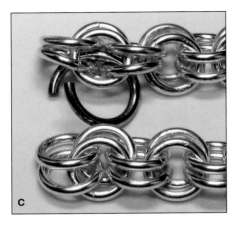
c

d

Process photos by Anne E. Mitchell.

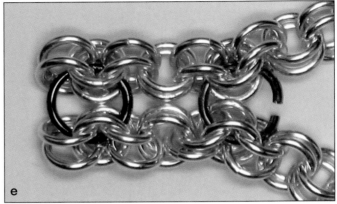
e

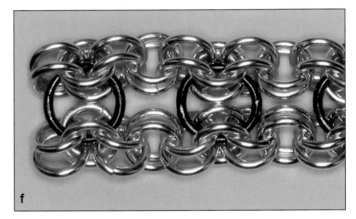
f

Do not close the large jump ring
[photo c].

► **4** Working on the lower chain,
insert the same large jump ring through
the upper ring of the third link pair,
then between the two rings of the
second link pair, and out through the
upper ring of the first link pair. Close
the large jump ring [photo d].

► **5** Insert a second large jump
ring into the upper chain, inserting it
through the lower ring of the fifth link
pair, then between the rings of the sixth
link pair, and out through the lower
ring of the seventh link pair. Weave the
same jump ring into the corresponding
link pairs in the bottom chain. Close
the large jump ring [photo e].

► **6** Note that you only skipped one
section, the fourth link pair, when you
added the second large jump ring. Skip
the eighth link pair, and weave the
third large jump ring in with the ninth,
tenth, and 11th link pairs on the top
chain, then on the bottom chain. Skip a
link pair after adding each large jump
ring. Continue with the pattern until
your chain is complete [photo f].

► **7** At one end of the chain, thread a
single small jump ring through each
two-link pair. Thread the single small
jump rings through the corresponding
loops of one half of a two-strand
magnetic slide clasp. Close the jump
rings. Repeat on the other end of
the chain.

Egyptian mystery

Coils are as alluring to us today as they have been to many cultures through the millennia. Repeat a single, easy coil link to make a dynamic chain.

designed by **Marie Cristine Knuff**

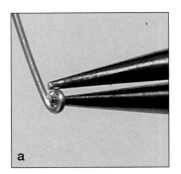

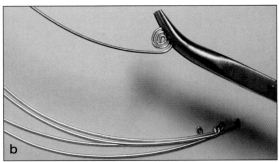

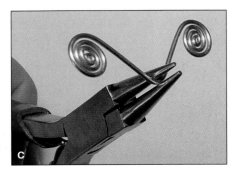

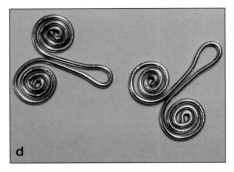

PROJECT NOTES:
• Don't attach the original link to the chain until all of the other links are connected. If you need to make a few more links to reach your desired length, you can use the original link as a guide to keep the new links consistent with the others.
• To make a necklace, count how many links are in 1 in. (2.5cm) of chain. Multiply that number of links by the number of inches (or millimeters) needed for the necklace.

The name of this coiled link is a bit of a mystery. Jewelry-history texts cite the link as Scandinavian in origin. In the 1940s, two Danish authors, who were influenced by a revival of Egyptian motifs, wrote a book on wire jewelry making and mythologized the link, attributing it to an ancient Egyptian goldsmith. From this text, we get the currently popular name — the Egyptian coil link.

Bracelet
► **1** Use flush cutters to cut 25 5-in. (13cm) pieces of 18-gauge sterling silver wire. File the ends flat.

► **2** Use the tip of your roundnose pliers to make a tight loop at each end of a piece of wire [photo a] so that the loops curl toward each other. Repeat for the remaining 24 wires.
► **3** Use flatnose or bentnose pliers to coil each end of the wire toward the other, making three-and-a-half turns [photo b]. Leave approximately ¾ in. (1.9cm) of straight wire between the two coils.
► **4** Use the first coiled wire as a guide for coiling the remaining 24 wires, making sure your coils are uniform in shape and size. You can also use a brass slide gauge or calipers to measure the coils, adjusting them as necessary to keep them consistent.

NOTE: For a different look, use a planishing hammer to flatten and texture the coils.

► **5** Use roundnose pliers to make a U bend in the wire halfway between the coils [photo c]. Make the space in the center of the bend 3mm (⅛ in.) wide. Squeeze the wires 5mm (¼ in.) from the U [photo d]. This will snug the wires while leaving space for another link to pass through the U. Repeat for each link.
► **6** Use roundnose pliers to grasp the wire at the base of the coils. Bend the U over until it is parallel to the coils,

creating a hook [photo e]. Adjust the wire so the hook is even on each side. Repeat for each link.
► **7** Thread the hook of one link under the coils and through the hook of another link [photo f]. Continue until all the links are connected. If your chain is crooked, gently but firmly pull the chain, one link at a time [photo g]. This will help to define and straighten the chain.
► **8** Starting at one end, place your index finger underneath the chain to support it while pressing the coils down [photo h]. This will make a slight peak in the middle of the chain [photo i].
► **9** Open a 3mm ID jump ring, and attach it to the hook at one end of the chain [photo j]. Close the jump ring. Attach two more jump rings, leaving the second one open. On the other end of the chain, attach a jump ring to the loop of the hook. Attach one half of the clasp to the jump ring on each end [photo k]. Close each jump ring.
► **10** Attach 5–9mm ID jump rings to the toggle loop, if desired, so the fit of the bracelet is adjustable [photo l]. Tumble polish or patinate the bracelet as desired.

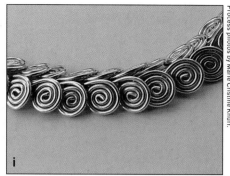

Process photos by Marie Cristine Knuff.

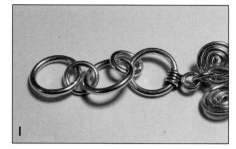

PROJECT NOTES:

To make a pair of earrings, make three coil links as you did for the bracelet.

materials

- 25 in. (64cm) 18-gauge round half-hard sterling silver wire
- 4 18-gauge, 5mm ID sterling silver jump rings
- pair of ear wires

1 Make a single-coil link by cutting a 2½-in. (64mm) piece of wire. On one end of the wire, make a coil as you did for the coil links. On the other end, grasp the wire 5mm (¼ in.) from the end, and bend the wire over the pliers to form a hook.

2 Connect the coil links to each other as you did for the bracelet. Attach the single-coil link by sliding its hook through the hook of the second coil link. Trim the excess wire with flush cutters.

3 Open a 5mm jump ring and attach it to the hook of the top coil link. Close the jump ring. Attach another 5mm jump ring to the same hook and through the first jump ring. Open the loop of an ear wire, attach both jump rings, and close the loop. Adjust the links with your fingers as you did to shape the chain. Make a second earring. Finish the earrings to match your chain.

MATERIALS

bracelet, 7½ in. (19.1cm)

- 11–12½ ft. (3.4–3.8m) 18-gauge round, dead-soft, sterling silver wire
- sterling silver jump rings
  - **4** 18-gauge (1.0mm), 3mm ID
  - **3–7** 18-gauge, 5–9mm ID (optional)
- toggle clasp
- bentnose pliers
- flatnose pliers
- roundnose pliers
- flush cutters
- hand or needle file
- brass slide gauge or calipers
- planishing hammer (optional)
- anvil (optional)
- finishing items (choose from): tumbler, steel shot, burnishing compound
- liver of sulfur
- polishing cloth

Materials note:

This bracelet uses 18-gauge round sterling silver wire, but you can use 20-gauge as well. The 6½-in. (16.5cm) bracelet is adjustable to 8 in. (20cm) if you add jump rings to the toggle clasp.

Whip up a
beautiful necklace

Use a mandrel to master this chain
mail pattern. Getting started is the
only tricky part about this chain; once
you've established the pattern, it's
quick and easy to make.

designed by Esther Lee

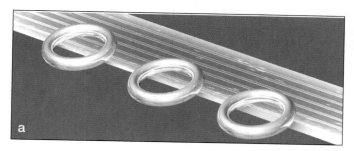

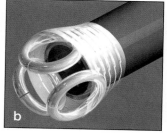

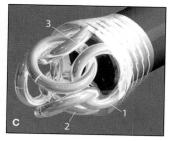

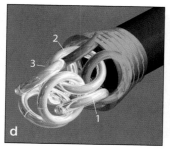

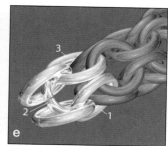

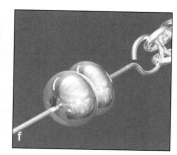

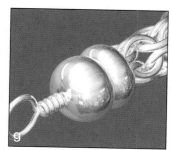

MATERIALS

necklace, 16 in. (41cm)

- 350 18-gauge 4.5–5mm ID sterling silver jump rings
- 8 in. (20cm) 18- or 20-gauge sterling silver wire
- 2 end caps
- S-hook clasp
- nylon-reinforced tape
- 8mm (⁵⁄₁₆-in.) diameter mandrel
- 2 pairs of chainnose pliers
- roundnose pliers
- jump ring maker (optional)
- wire cutters

Materials note:

For this project, the designer made her own jump rings, using half-hard wire wound around a 4mm (⁵⁄₃₂-in.) mandrel; due to the "spring" factor, the inside diameter (ID) of her finished jump rings is larger than the size of the mandrel she wound them on. If you're buying premade jump rings, get jump rings that have an ID of **4.5mm** or **5mm**.

PROJECT NOTE:

To add your own personal touch to prefabricated S-hook clasps, try using a planishing hammer and a bench block to flatten the center part of the S-hook. Or, slide a bead to the center of the S, and then flatten the hooks.

Necklace

► **1** Cut a piece of ¼-in. (6.5mm) nylon-reinforced tape, approximately 1½ in. (3.8cm) long. Place the tape sticky-side up on your work surface. Close three jump rings, and place them on the tape so that half of each ring extends above the tape **[photo a]**. Press the rings firmly to the tape so that they stick. Wrap the tape around the end of an 8mm (⁵⁄₁₆-in.) mandrel **[photo b]** so that the exposed ends of the rings extend above the mandrel.

TIPS: If you have a jump ring maker, you can use one of the steel mandrels that came as part of the set. You can also use a ballpoint pen or a wooden dowel (for this project, a segment cut from an 8mm (U.S. size 11) aluminum knitting needle). The size of your mandrel is determined by the size of the rings you're using; three rings should fit evenly around the mandrel's perimeter. If you're using larger rings, you'll need a larger mandrel.

► **2** Open nine jump rings. Use a ring to connect rings 1 and 2, another ring to connect rings 2 and 3, and a third ring to connect rings 3 and 1 **[photo c]**.

► **3** Repeat, using a ring to connect the new rings 1 and 2, another ring to connect rings 2 and 3, and another ring to connect rings 3 and 1 **[photo d]**. Continue adding rings in sets of three until the chain is the desired length.

► **4** To end this chain with end caps and an S-hook clasp, taper the ends from three to two rings. First, open four rings. Thread a ring through rings 1 and 2 at the end of the chain, and close it. Thread another ring through rings 2 and 3, and close it **[photo e]**. If desired, thread a ring through the two end rings, and close it; repeat with a second ring. Repeat to taper the other end of the chain.

► **5** Cut a 4-in. (10cm) piece of 18- or 20-gauge wire. Use roundnose pliers to make a plain loop at one end of the wire. Thread the loop through the two jump rings at the end of your chain, and close the loop. Slide an end cap onto the wire **[photo f]**, and make a wrapped loop **[photo g]**. Repeat to add an end cap to the opposite end of the chain.

► **6** Use an S-hook clasp to connect the two wrapped loops.

Perfect
pairing

Full Persian chain mail sections frame lampworked focal beads in this collaboration between a jewelry designer and lampwork artist.

designed by Kathy Petersen and Susan Matych-Hager

a

b

c

d

e

f

g

h

Focal-bead centerpiece

► **1** Cut a 4-in. (10cm) piece of wire, and make a plain loop.

► **2** String the beads as desired. Bend the wire to fit the curve of your wrist. Make a plain loop on the other end, and trim the wire. Set the centerpiece aside.

Chain mail sections

► **1** Close four of the 7mm jump rings and open the remaining 7mm jump rings.

► **2** Slide an open 7mm jump ring through the four closed jump rings, and close it. Slide another 7mm jump ring through the four closed jump rings, and close it. Split the group of four jump rings into two sets of two [photo a].

► **3** Position the six-ring chain so that the first and last pairs of jump rings are parallel to the work surface. The center pair of jump rings will stand upright [photo b].

► **4** Slide the top right-hand jump ring over the top left-hand jump ring, and the bottom right-hand jump ring under the bottom left-hand jump ring, sandwiching the left-hand jump rings between the right-hand jump rings. Insert a pin between the upright pair of jump rings to hold the horizontal jump rings in place [photo c].

► **5** Following the path created by the pin, slide a 7mm jump ring between the upright jump rings and over the horizontal jump rings, and close the jump ring [photo d]. Slide a second 7mm jump ring next to the one added in this step, and close the jump ring [photo e].

► **6** Turn the chain a quarter turn so that the jump rings added in the previous step are parallel to your work surface. Slide a 7mm jump ring to one side of the upright jump rings, and close it [photo f]. Slide a 7mm jump ring to the other side of the upright jump rings, and close it [photo g].

► **7** Turn the chain a quarter turn so that the jump rings added in the previous step are parallel to your work surface.

► **8** Repeat steps 4–7 for the desired length of the chain. Make a second chain.

Assembly

► **1** Open the two jump rings on the starting end of one section of chain. Attach a loop of the centerpiece to the jump rings, positioning it between the vertical jump rings, and close the jump rings [photo h]. Repeat with the other section of chain.

► **2** Adjust the length of your bracelet as needed, adding or removing 7mm jump rings.

► **3** Open two 5mm jump rings. Slide each jump ring between the vertical jump rings of the working end and over the horizontal jump rings, attaching half of the clasp. Close the jump rings [photo i]. Repeat on the other end of the bracelet.

i

MATERIALS

bracelet, 7¾ in. (19.7 cm)
- 35mm lampworked focal bead
- **2** 6mm lampworked spacer beads
- **4–6** sterling silver spacer beads
- clasp with horizontal connection rings
- 4 in. (10cm) 16-gauge sterling silver wire, half-hard
- sterling silver jump rings
  - **160** 7mm OD 18-gauge
  - **4** 5mm OD, 18-gauge
- corsage or T-pin
- chainnose pliers
- roundnose pliers
- wire cutters

Materials note:

Each chain mail section is 2½ in. (6.4cm) long. The beads and spacers were created by lampwork artist Susan Matych-Hager.

PROJECT NOTE:
Colored anodized aluminum jump rings were used for the how-to photographs. These jump rings are also larger than the sterling silver jump rings used in the bracelets.

Patchwork
principle

Mimic a quilt's patchwork pattern by making each round
a different color. Form a bracelet by connecting the
units with additional colored jump rings.
For a classic look, use sterling silver
and gold-filled jump rings.

designed by Amanda Shero Granstrom

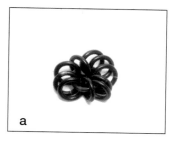

a

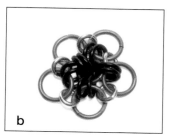

b

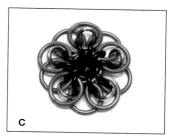

c

d

e

f

g

h

Jump ring units

You will need five color A and 10 color B 6.4mm jump rings, one color C 4.8mm jump ring, 10 color C and 10 color D 4mm jump rings, and five color E 3.2mm jump rings for each unit.

▶ **1** Open one C 4.8mm jump ring, attach eight closed C 4mm jump rings, and close the jump ring. Open two more C 4mm jump rings, attach them to the 4.8mm jump ring, and close them [photo a].

▶ **2** Open five A 6.4mm jump rings, and close five E 3.2mm jump rings.

▶ **3** Slide an A 6.4mm jump ring through two of the C 4mm jump rings on the 4.8mm jump ring. Attach an E 3.2mm jump ring on each side of the A 6.4mm jump ring. Close the A 6.4mm jump ring.

▶ **4** Slide an A 6.4mm jump ring through the next two C 4mm jump rings and one of the attached E 3.2mm jump rings. Attach one closed E 3.2mm jump ring to the new A 6.4mm jump ring. Close the A 6.4mm jump ring.

▶ **5** Repeat step 4 three times. Slide the last A 6.4mm jump ring through the last two C 4mm jump rings and the two adjacent E 3.2mm jump rings, and close the jump ring [photo b].

▶ **6** Open 10 color B 6.4mm jump rings.

▶ **7** Slide a B 6.4mm jump ring through two C 4mm jump rings from adjacent pairs. Close the jump ring. Repeat four times [photo c]. Flip the unit, and repeat on the opposite side

[photo d]. Flex the finished unit so that the jump rings added in step 2 lie evenly around the center jump ring.

▶ **8** Repeat steps 1–7 six times to make a total of seven units.

Assembly

▶ **1** Open 70 color D 4mm jump rings.

▶ **2** Slide an open D 4mm jump ring through the intersection of the one A and two B 6.4mm jump rings, and one A 6.4mm jump ring of another unit. Close the D 4mm jump ring. Repeat, sliding another D 4mm jump ring through the adjacent intersection of the A and B 6.4mm jump rings and the same A jump ring of the other unit [photo e].

▶ **3** Repeat step 2 to connect the remaining units.

▶ **4** After the units are joined, add eight D 4mm jump rings to each unit, sliding a D 4mm jump ring through each color A and B 6.4mm intersection, as in step 2 [photo f].

▶ **5** Open the 3.2 and 4mm aluminum jump rings.

▶ **6** Slide an open 3.2mm jump ring through two D 4mm jump rings on one end of the bracelet. Close the jump ring. Work a 1+1 chain of 4mm jump rings from the 3.2mm jump ring. Close the end jump ring [photo g].

▶ **7** Slide an open 3.2mm jump ring through the A 6.4mm jump ring on the other end of the bracelet and attach the clasp. Close the jump ring [photo h].

MATERIALS

bracelet, 7½ in. (19.1cm)
- anodized aluminum jump rings, each size in a different color
  - 6.4mm ID 18-gauge, **35** color A, **70** color B
  - 7 4.8mm ID 18-gauge, color C
  - 4mm ID 18-gauge, **70** color C, **70** color D
- **35** 3.2mm ID 18-gauge, color E
- aluminum jump rings for clasp
  - **8–12** 4mm ID 18-gauge
  - **2** 3.2mm ID 18-gauge
- 10mm lobster claw clasp
- bentnose pliers
- chainnose pliers

Lampwork
links

Use a variation of Byzantine chain to show off a collection of small focal beads. Art-glass beads are perfect for this design, though other large-hole focal beads work well, too.

designed by Kathy Petersen and Susan Matych-Hager

a

b

c

d

e

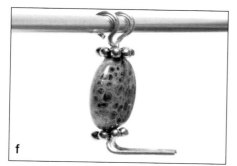

f

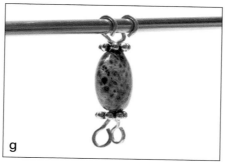

g

MATERIALS

bracelet, 7 in. (18cm)

- **3–5** art-glass beads or other large-hole focal beads (you need to be able to fit two thicknesses of wire through the beads)
- **2** art-glass spacer beads (optional)
- **6–10** metal spacers
- **2-strand** clasp
- **120** 6mm outside-diameter jump rings, 18-gauge
- **18–30 in.** (46–76cm) 18–20-gauge wire, half-hard
- **6mm** knitting needle or dowel (optional)
- bentnose pliers
- chainnose pliers
- roundnose pliers
- wire cutters

Material notes:

Mistletoe beads by Susan Matych-Hager, mottled green borosilicate lentils by Unicorne Beads (unicornebeads.com).

Bead components

► **1** Place a 6mm jump ring on one jaw of your roundnose pliers, and mark where it sits with a marker [photo a]. This mark indicates where you should place the wire in the following steps in order to make the loops the same size as the jump rings.

► **2** Cut a 3–4-in. (7.6–10cm) piece of wire, place one end of the wire at the mark made in step 1, and make a plain loop [photo b].

► **3** Grasp the loop with your chainnose pliers, and make a right-angle bend [photo c].

► **4** Grasp the wire right after the bend, and make another right-angle bend going away from the loop [photo d].

► **5** Repeat steps 2–4 with another wire, but make the first bend in the opposite direction so the loops are parallel and sit about ⅜ in. (1cm) apart when the long ends of the wire come together in the middle.

► **6** Over both wires, string one or more spacers, a focal bead, and one or more spacers. Bend the wire ends in opposite directions [photo e]. At this point, you may find it helpful to slide a knitting needle or dowel through the loops. This will stabilize them as you complete the bead component.

► **7** Grasp one wire right next to the bend made in step 6, and bend it in the opposite direction of the cut part of the loop on the other end. Repeat with the other wire. Trim the wires to about ⅝ in. (1.6cm) [photo f]. With roundnose pliers, make a loop with one of the wires. Repeat with the other wire [photo g].

► **8** Repeat steps 2–7 with the remaining focal beads.

h

i

j

k

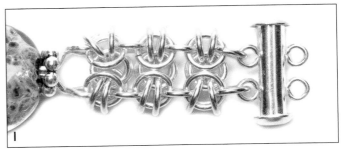

l

Chain mail sections

► **1** Open four and close six 6mm jump rings. On an open jump ring, attach four closed jump rings, and close it. Slide another open jump ring through the four closed jump rings, and close it. This creates a 2+2+2 chain.

► **2** Slide an open jump ring through an end pair of jump rings, attach the remaining two closed rings, and close the open jump ring. Slide the remaining open jump ring through the four jump rings the previous open ring went through, and close it. This creates a chain of 10 rings, attached in pairs [photo h].

► **3** Repeat steps 1 and 2.

► **4** Flip the end pair of rings on one chain back toward the rest of the chain. Repeat with an end pair of rings on the other chain. Open a jump ring, and slide it through the side of each set of flipped rings. Close the ring [photo i].

► **5** Repeat step 4 at the other end of the chains [photo j].

► **6** Repeat steps 1–5 until you have one more chain mail section than you have bead components.

Assembly

► **1** Open a loop of a bead component, and slide it through a pair of flipped rings on a chain mail section, on the side opposite the jump ring that connected the two chains. Close the loop.

► **2** To connect the other loop of the component to the remaining pair of flipped rings of the chain mail section, open one of the flipped rings, guide it through the loop, and close the ring. Repeat with the other ring [photo k]. This is the most challenging part of this project, and you may need a little extra patience and persistence to get these rings properly positioned.

► **3** Repeat steps 1 and 2 to connect the remaining chain mail sections and bead components.

► **4** Test for fit, and add or remove a 10-ring section of chain mail from each end if needed. To add a section, repeat steps 1 and 2 of "Chain mail sections," then connect it to one end of the bracelet as in steps 4 and 5.

► **5** To attach the clasp, open a jump ring, slide it through two end flipped rings and a loop of half of the clasp, and close the ring. Repeat with the other loop of the clasp [photo l].

► **6** Repeat step 5 at the other end of the bracelet.

Basic **addition**

Use a simple chain as a foundation for a bold new pattern; three
chains join into one, creating a pattern that is sturdy and dense,

a

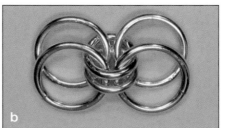

b

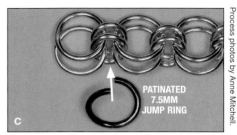

c

PATINATED
7.5MM
JUMP RING

d

f

e

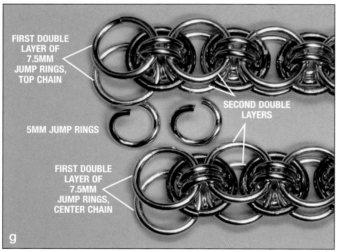

FIRST DOUBLE
LAYER OF
7.5MM
JUMP RINGS,
TOP CHAIN

SECOND DOUBLE
LAYERS

5MM JUMP RINGS

FIRST DOUBLE
LAYER OF
7.5MM
JUMP RINGS,
CENTER CHAIN

g

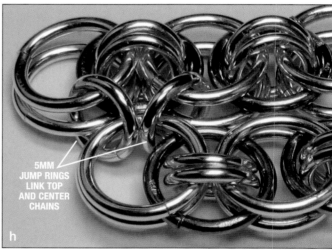

5MM
JUMP RINGS
LINK TOP
AND CENTER
CHAINS

h

5MM
JUMP RINGS
LINK CENTER
AND BOTTOM
CHAINS

i

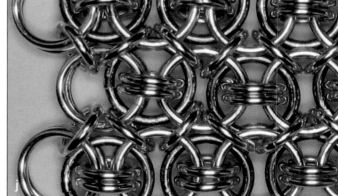

j

The basic chain is a classic Japanese overlay—a dense pattern that lends itself well to a bracelet or choker. Once you've made three rows of Japanese overlay, you'll connect them with a crisscross pattern of smaller jump rings, and the resulting chain mail will have enough rigidity to sustain its width while maintaining the fluidity that chain mail is known for.

► **1** Close 34 7.5mm jump rings, and open 32 5mm jump rings.

► **2** Construct a 2+2+2 chain, which is a simple sequence of pairs of jump rings, by alternating pairs of closed 7.5mm jump rings with pairs of open 5mm jump rings [photos a, b]. Repeat to create a second 2+2+2 chain.

► **3** Create a third 2+2+2 chain by closing 32 7.5mm jump rings and 30 5mm jump rings. This chain is just one section shorter; the difference in length will create the offset pattern.

► **4** Patinate a total of 47 7.5mm jump rings. Open the patinated jump rings [photo c], but not too much, as it will make weaving them into the chains more difficult.

► **5** Place one of the long, completed chains on the work surface. Slide a patinated jump ring around the first

pair of 5mm jump rings in the chain, in between the two layers of 7.5mm jump rings. Close the patinated jump ring [photos d and e]. Continue to the end of the chain. Use the remaining patinated jump rings for the two remaining 2+2+2 chains.

► **6** Place the three completed overlay chains on the work surface. Put the shorter chain in between the two longer chains, and offset it one link [photo f].

► **7** Open 64 5mm jump rings [photo g].

► **8** Slide a 5mm jump ring vertically through the first double layer of 7.5mm jump rings in the top chain, then through the first double layer of 7.5mm jump rings in the center chain. Close the 5mm jump ring. Slide a 5mm jump ring through the second double layer of 7.5mm jump rings in the top chain, then through the first double layer of 7.5mm jump rings in the center chain. Close the 5mm jump ring. Make sure that the 5mm jump rings capture only the non-patinated jump rings [photo h].

► **9** Repeat step 8 to connect the center overlay chain to the bottom overlay chain [photo i]. Repeat to the end of the chain [photo j].

MATERIALS
bracelet, 7⅝ x 1⅛ in. (19.4 x 2.9cm)

- jump rings
  - **147** (2 oz. troy) 16-gauge, 7.5mm ID
  - **158** (1.5 oz. troy) 16-gauge, 5mm ID
- large two-strand toggle clasp
- bentnose pliers
- chainnose pliers
- padded work surface
- liver of sulfur
- steel wool (optional)

Supply note:
Handmade metal clay toggle clasp by Kate McKinnon.

PROJECT NOTE:
Choose your clasp carefully. A two-strand clasp with a good heft works nicely. Small jump rings anchor the clasp to the center layer of patinated jump rings.

Ruffled
rings

Create colorful dangling earrings from layered jump ring clusters. A gorgeous clustered effect that results from combining jump rings in different sizes and wire gauges. Beads and crystals add extra sparkle to the jump rings and earring findings.

Designed by Sandy Amazeen

PROJECT NOTE:
If you use smaller jump rings of a finer wire gauge, you will need to stack more jump rings on each side of the base jump ring to fill it out.

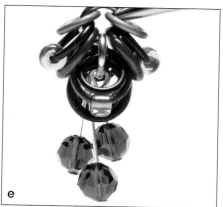

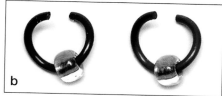

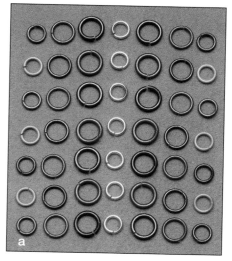

You can make these earrings from any combination of jump rings — vary the jump ring size, wire gauge, and color. Customize them even more by changing the length, dangling crystals or beads from the bottom, or embellishing the jump rings with beads. Follow these basic instructions, and modify them as desired.

► **1** For each earring, you will need seven 4.25mm stainless steel or brass jump rings for the base chain, and three sets of 14 rings in different sizes, wire gauges, and/or colors. Select your jump rings, and lay them on your work surface in rows with the base jump rings in the middle and symmetrical rows on each side [photo a].

► **2** Open the seven base jump rings and close the remaining jump rings. If you plan to attach a seed bead to any of the jump rings, do this before closing the jump rings [photo b].

► **3** If you plan to attach dangles to the bottom of the earrings, make them now. To make a dangle, string a 6mm crystal on a head or eye pin. Note the

size of the bottom jump ring before making a plain loop. Make the loop large enough to fit around the jump ring. Vary the length of the dangles if you are adding more than one. Slide the bottom base jump ring through the plain loops before you attach the sets of jump rings [photo c].

► **4** Attach a set of closed jump rings to an open base jump ring in the order they were placed on your work surface, working from the center outward. Repeat to attach the remaining set of jump rings from that row [photo d]. Close the base jump ring.

► **5** Slide an open base jump ring through the top of the closed base jump ring. Attach the sets of closed jump rings on each side of the base jump ring. Close the base jump ring [photo e].

► **6** Repeat step 5 with the remaining open base jump rings.

► **7** Attach an ear wire to the top base jump ring [photo f].

► **8** Make a second earring.

MATERIALS
pair of earrings
- 2–6 6–8mm crystals (optional)
- 12–14 size 6º or 8º seed beads (optional)
- 2–6 2-in. (5cm) 20-gauge head pins or eye pins (optional)
- jump rings
  - 14 4.25mm ID stainless steel or brass, 18-gauge
  - 84 anodized aluminum in assorted colors sizes/wire gauges
- pair of ear wires
- bentnose pliers
- chainnose pliers
- roundnose pliers (optional)
- wire cutters (optional)

PROJECT NOTE:
If closing the base jump ring is difficult, remove one of the colored jump rings, and close the base jump ring. Open the colored jump ring, and slide it through the base jump ring.

Jump ring flowers

Take a flower base with multiple petals and give it some glitz with your choice of crystal, pearl, or glass-bead dangles. Vary the dangle length or leave the chain mail center unembellished.

designed by Deanna Kittrell

FIGURE 1

FIGURE 2

FIGURE 3

FIGURE 4

FIGURE 5

FIGURE 6

FIGURE 7

Jump ring base

▶ **1** Open 14 5mm jump rings, and close 24 3mm jump rings. Attach 12 closed 3mm jump rings to one of the 5mm jump rings. Close the jump ring [figure 1]. Slide a second 5mm jump ring through the 3mm jump rings, so that it sits on top of the first. The second 5mm jump rings added in each step are not shown in the illustrations.

▶ **2** Slide a 5mm jump ring through two adjacent 3mm jump rings. Attach four 3mm jump rings to the 5mm. Close the jump ring [figure 2]. Slide a second 5mm jump ring through the six 3mm jump rings joined in this step.

▶ **3** Continuing around the center jump ring, slide a 5mm jump ring through two of the 3mm jump rings added in the previous step and the next two 3mm jump rings attached to the center 5mm jump ring. Attach two 3mm jump rings [figure 3]. Slide a second 5mm jump ring through the 3mm jump rings joined in this step. Repeat three times [figures 4–6].

▶ **4** To complete the flower, slide a 5mm jump ring through the six remaining 3mm jump rings [figure 7]. Slide a second 5mm jump ring through the 3mm jump rings joined in this step.

▶ **5** Make a second flower.

Embellishment

▶ **1** On a head pin, string a 6mm bicone crystal and a 4mm bicone crystal, and make a wrapped loop.

▶ **2** Cut a 3-in. (7.6cm) piece of wire. At one end, make the first half of a wrapped loop. Slide the head pin dangle into the unfinished loop. Complete the wraps, and trim the wire. String a 4mm, a 6mm, and a 4mm onto the wire, and make a wrapped loop.

▶ **3** Open a 4mm jump ring, attach the dangle, and slide the 4mm jump ring through a pair of 5mm jump rings at the base of the earring. Close the jump ring.

▶ **4** Repeat steps 1–3 to make two more dangles, attaching the dangles to the 5mms adjacent to the ones to which you attached the first dangle.

▶ **5** Attach an ear wire with a 4mm jump ring or a bead-embellished dangle with wrapped loops on each end.

▶ **6** Repeat steps 1–5 to embellish the other earring.

MATERIALS
earrings
- bicone crystals
  - **14** 6mm
  - **18** 4mm
- 24 in. (61cm) 22-gauge sterling silver wire, half-hard
- **6** 22-gauge head pins
- sterling silver jump rings
  - **28** 5mm ID, 16-gauge
  - **6–8** 4mm ID, 18-gauge
  - **48** 3mm ID, 20-gauge
- pair of ear wires
- bentnose pliers
- chainnose pliers
- roundnose pliers
- wire cutters

PROJECT NOTES:
• The second-layer jump rings fit very snugly. To make inserting them easier, only open the jump ring about 1/16 in. (2mm).
• Feed the end that is flush with your work surface through the opening.
• Grasp the jump ring from the back, opposite the end you are feeding through the opening.

2 quick earrings

Take time to add two pairs of chain mail earrings to your collection. They go with everything and can be embellished with crystals for added sparkle.

designed by Deanna Kittrell

FIGURE 1

FIGURE 2

FIGURE 3

FIGURE 4

FIGURE 5

FIGURE 6

DAISY CHAIN

MATERIALS

both projects
- bentnose pliers
- chainnose pliers
- roundnose pliers
- wire cutters

triangle earrings
- bicone crystals
  - **16** 6mm
  - **12** 4mm
- 26 in. (66 cm) 22-gauge sterling silver wire, half-hard
- 6 head pins, 22-gauge
- sterling silver jump rings
  - **24** 5mm ID, 16-gauge
  - **6–8** 4mm ID, 20-gauge
  - **36** 3mm ID, 20-gauge
- pair of ear wires

daisy chain earrings
- crystals
  - **2** 8mm round
  - **2** 6mm bicone
  - **2** 4mm bicone
- 2 bead caps for 8mm crystals
- 6 in. (15 cm) 22-gauge sterling silver wire, half-hard
- 2 head pins, 22-gauge
- sterling silver jump rings
- **22** 5mm ID, 16-gauge
- **2** 4mm ID, 20-gauge
- pair of ear wires

Triangle earrings
Base
► **1** Open 12 5mm jump rings, and close 18 3mm jump rings. Attach four closed 3mm jump rings to one of the 5mm jump rings. Close the jump ring [figure 1]. Slide a second 5mm jump ring through the 3mm jump rings, so that it is on top of the first. Close the second jump ring. The second 5mm jump rings added in each step are not shown in the illustrations.
► **2** Slide a 5mm jump ring through a pair of 3mm jump rings from step 1. Attach six 3mm jump rings. Close the jump ring [figure 2]. Slide another 5mm jump ring through the eight 3mm jump rings joined in this step.
► **3** Slide a 5mm jump ring through the remaining 3mm jump rings on the first 5mm jump ring and the two nearest 3mm jump rings on the adjacent 5mm jump ring. Attach four 3mm jump rings. Close the jump ring [figure 3]. Slide a second 5mm jump ring through the eight 3mm jump rings joined in this step.
► **4** Slide a 5mm jump ring through two edge 3mm jump rings, and attach two 3mm jump rings. Close the jump ring [figure 4]. Slide a second 5mm jump ring through the four 3mm jump rings joined in this step.
► **5** Slide a 5mm jump ring through the six 3mm jump rings on adjacent 5mm jump rings. Attach two 3mm jump rings. Close the jump ring [figure 5]. Slide a second 5mm jump ring through the eight 3mm jump rings joined in this step.
► **6** Slide a 5mm jump ring through the four 3mm jump rings on adjacent 5mm jump rings. Close the jump ring [figure 6]. Slide a second 5mm jump ring through the four 3mm jump rings joined in this step.
► **7** Open a 4mm jump ring, and attach it to an earring finding and the pair of 5mm jump rings at the top of the earring. Alternatively, cut a 3-in. (7.6cm) piece of wire, and make the first half of a wrapped loop one end. Slide the top pair of 5mm jump rings into the loop, complete the wraps, and trim the wire. String a 6mm bicone crystal, and make a wrapped loop. Open the loop of an ear wire, attach it to the wrapped loop, and close it.
► **8** Make a second earring.

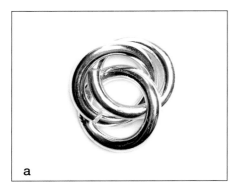

a

b

Embellishment

▶ **1** On a head pin, string a 6mm and a 4mm bicone crystal, and make a wrapped loop.

▶ **2** Cut a 3-in. (7.6cm) piece of wire, and make the first half of a wrapped loop. Slide the head pin dangle into the loop. Complete the wraps, and trim the wire. String a 6mm and a 4mm onto the wire, and make a wrapped loop.

▶ **3** Open a 4mm jump ring, attach the dangle, and slide the 4mm jump ring through a pair of 5mm jump rings at the base corner of the triangle. Close the jump ring.

▶ **4** Repeat steps 1–3 to make a second dangle, and attach it to the pair of 5mm jump rings at the other base corner of the triangle.

▶ **5** Repeat steps 1 and 2. Make a third unit with one 6mm, and attach it to the top of the second unit. Repeat step 3 to attach the three-unit dangle to the pair of 5mm jump rings at the base center of the triangle.

▶ **6** Repeat steps 1–5 with the other earring.

PROJECT NOTE:

The second-layer 5mm jump ring fits very snugly. To make inserting it easier, only open the jump ring about 1/16 in. (2mm). Feed the end that is flush with your work surface through the opening. Grasp the jump ring from the back, opposite the end you are feeding through the opening.

Daisy chain earrings
Base

▶ **1** Open eight and close three 5mm jump rings.

▶ **2** Attach a closed 5mm jump ring to an open 5mm jump ring. Close the jump ring. Slide an open 5mm jump ring through the two closed jump rings. Close the jump ring [photo a]. Repeat twice to make three jump ring clusters.

▶ **3** Slide an open 5mm jump ring through two jump ring clusters [photo b]. Close the jump ring. Repeat to attach the third jump ring cluster to one of the connected clusters.

▶ **4** Attach an ear wire with a 4mm jump ring, or a bead-embellished dangle as in step 7 of "Triangle earrings."

▶ **5** Make a second earring.

Embellishment

▶ **1** On a head pin, string an 8mm round crystal, a bead cap, and a 6mm bicone crystal, and make the first half of a wrapped loop.

▶ **2** Slide the bottom jump ring cluster of the earring into the loop of the head pin dangle. Complete the wraps, and trim the wire.

▶ **3** Repeat steps 1 and 2 with the other earring.

Links to
Atlantis

Nestle ocean jasper beads between Byzantine links for a handmade silver bracelet with a subtle splash of color. The difference in length between the links gives the edges of this bracelet a wavy look.

designed by Phyllis Adams

 a

 b

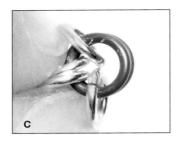 c

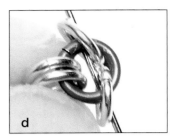 d

 e

 f

 g

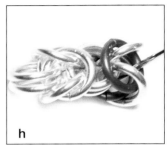 h

Ocean jasper displays a beautiful range of colors, including greens, whites, yellows, and sometimes pinks. Contrasting dots, rings, and streaks mean every bead is different from the next. Choose your beads carefully as you make this bracelet, and, between admiring the beads and appreciating the chain mail, you may find yourself lost in another world.

Byzantine crossbar links

In the process photos, the rings being added are shown in blue for visibility.

▶ **1** Open 10 and close four jump rings.

▶ **2** Attach the four closed jump rings to an open jump ring, and close it [photo a]. Repeat to attach a second jump ring to the four closed jump rings. Position the rings as a 2+2+2 chain [photo b].

▶ **3** Flip the far right pair of rings back, so they sandwich the other end pair [photo c].

▶ **4** Spread the new end pair of jump rings apart, insert a pin between the spread rings, and slide it through the flipped pair [photo d]. This creates the space where you will insert your next jump ring.

▶ **5** Remove the pin, making sure to keep the space created by it open, and slide an open jump ring through the gap [photo e]. Close the jump ring. Repeat to add a second parallel jump ring.

▶ **6** Slide an open jump ring through the new pair of jump rings, and close it. Repeat to add a second parallel jump ring [photo f].

▶ **7** Repeat step 6 [photo g].

▶ **8** Flip the new pair of rings back, and insert the pin through the flipped rings as in steps 3 and 4 [photo h]. Repeat step 5 [photo i] to add the final pair of rings to the crossbar.

▶ **9** Repeat steps 1–8 15 times for a total of 16 crossbars.

Stone inserts

▶ **1** Cut a 1-in. (2.5cm) piece of wire, and make a plain loop on one end. String an 8mm disk bead, and make another plain loop [photo j].

▶ **2** Open a jump ring, slide it through one of the loops, and close it. Repeat with another jump ring [photo k].

▶ **3** Repeat step 2, attaching two jump rings to the other loop [photo l].

▶ **4** Repeat steps 1–3 six times to make a total of seven stone inserts.

Band assembly

▶ **1** Open four jump rings.

▶ **2** Slide an open jump ring through a pair of rings at the end of two crossbars, and close the ring [photo m]. Repeat to add a second parallel jump ring between the crossbars.

▶ **3** Repeat step 2 at the other end of the pair of crossbars [photo n].

▶ **4** Repeat steps 1–3 until you have eight connected pairs of crossbar units.

▶ **5** Open four jump rings.

▶ **6** Slide a ring through the pair of rings at the top right of a connected crossbar unit and the top pair of rings attached to a stone insert. Close the ring. Repeat to add a second parallel ring [photo o].

▶ **7** Repeat step 6 to connect the bottom right of the connected crossbar unit with the bottom of the stone insert.

▶ **8** Open four jump rings.

▶ **9** Slide a ring through the rings at the top of the stone insert from the previous step and the left top pair of rings of a new crossbar unit. Close the ring. Repeat to add a second parallel ring.

▶ **10** Repeat step 9 to connect the bottom of the stone insert to the bottom left of the connected crossbar unit [photo p].

▶ **11** Repeat steps 5–10 until you have connected all the stone inserts and connected crossbar units in an alternating pattern. End with a connected crossbar unit.

i

j

k

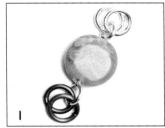

l

m

n

o

p

q

MATERIALS

bracelet, 7 in. (18cm)

- **7** 8mm gemstone disk- or coin-shaped beads, ocean jasper
- **388** 3–3.2mm ID jump rings, 20-gauge
- 2-strand tube clasp
- 7 in. (18cm) 20-gauge wire, half-hard
- liver of sulfur (optional)
- quilter's pin or equivalent
- tumbler (optional)
- bentnose pliers
- chainnose pliers
- roundnose pliers
- wire cutters

Clasp and finishing

▶ **1** Open four and close four jump rings, and connect them into a 2+2+2+2 chain. Open a jump ring, and slide it through a top end pair of rings at one end of the bracelet and an end pair of rings in the chain. Repeat with a second parallel ring.

▶ **2** Repeat step 1, but connect the chain to the bottom end pair of rings.

▶ **3** Open a jump ring, slide it through an end pair of rings and a loop of one half of the clasp, and close the ring. Repeat with a second parallel ring [photo q].

▶ **4** Repeat step 3 to connect the other chain to the other loop of the clasp.

▶ **5** Repeat steps 1–4 on the other end of the bracelet.

▶ **6** If desired, prepare a liver of sulfur solution according to the manufacturer's instructions. Tumble-polish to the desired finish.

PROJECT NOTE:

Using a pin to create the space for subsequent jump rings in the Byzantine chain is useful when you learn the chain mail pattern, but you may not need the pin once you understand how the weave works.

2 metals, 2 patterns

Make a streamlined flat-weave bracelet (gold-filled zigzag optional). A deceptively simple chain mail pattern forms the backbone for a zigzag variation. By using contrasting silver and gold-filled jump rings, you'll draw attention to the interwoven zigzag and give the basic flat bracelet added dimension.

designed by John Fetvedt

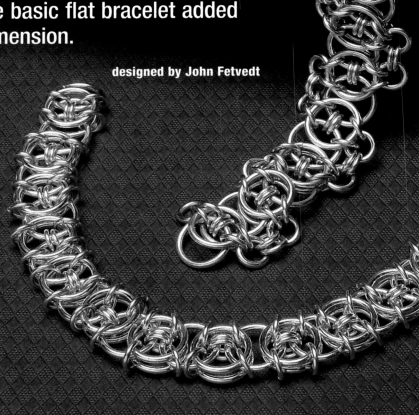

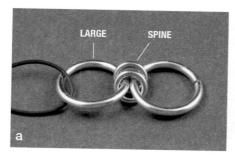

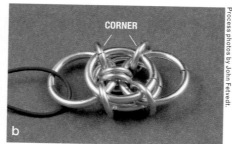

Process photos by John Fetvedt.

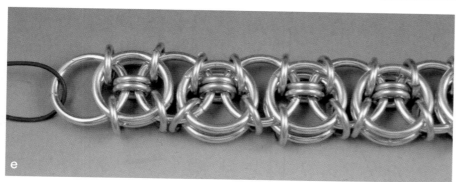

MATERIALS

zigzag variation bracelet,
8½ x ¾ in. (21.6 x 1.9cm). Its
streamlined cousin is 8½ x 9⁄16 in.
(21.6 x 1.4cm).
basic pattern

- **52** large 16-gauge 8mm ID
  sterling silver or Argentium
  sterling silver jump rings
- gold-filled jump rings
  - **34** spine jump rings,
    18-gauge, 3.2mm ID
  - **68** corner jump rings,
    18-gauge, 4mm ID
  - **3** small jump rings 18-gauge,
    3mm ID
- 18mm sterling silver toggle

**zigzag variation (materials
above plus)**

- gold-filled jump rings
  - **32** spine jump rings,
    18-gauge, 3.2mm ID
  - **34** zigzag jump rings,
    16-gauge, 4mm ID

Both projects

- 2 pairs of chainnose or flatnose
  pliers

For the understated look of the basic pattern, stop after part 1 and add a clasp to your chain. For the zigzag treatment, follow the steps in part 2.

Basic Celtic visions pattern

▶ **1** Twist a piece of scrap wire through an 8mm (large) jump ring. Use two 3.2mm (spine) jump rings to attach this large ring and a second large ring [photo a].

▶ **2** Sandwich the spine rings between two large jump rings. Thread and close four 4mm (corner) jump rings through the sandwich as shown [photo b].

▶ **3** Use two spine rings to connect another large ring to the end of the chain [photo c].

▶ **4** Repeat step 2 [photo d].

▶ **5** Continue the pattern to complete a chain to your desired length [photo e].

▶ **6** Optional: At one end of the chain, add a 1+1+1 series of 3mm jump rings, and attach the toggle half of a clasp. The large ring at the opposite end of the chain serves as the other half of the clasp.

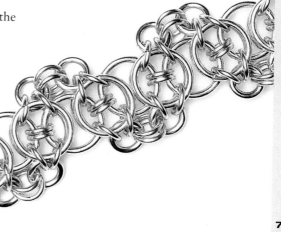

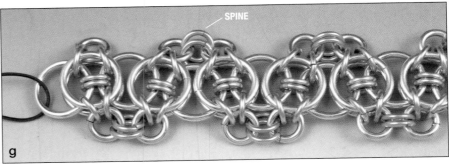

Zigzag variation

To make this variation, you'll build on the chain you made in "Basic Celtic visions pattern."

► **1** Starting at one end of the chain, use a 4 mm (zigzag) jump ring to connect each pair of corner jump rings [photo f].

► **2** Starting at one end of the chain, use two spine rings to connect two adjacent zigzag rings. Alternating sides of the chain, continue to connect all the remaining adjacent zigzag rings [photo g].

NOTE: You'll have a lone zigzag ring at each end of your chain.

► **3** At one end of the chain, add a 1+1+1 series of 3mm jump rings, and attach the toggle half of a clasp. The large ring at the opposite end of the chain serves as the other half of the clasp [photo h].

NOTE: To make this chain mail design more durable, you can fuse or solder the 8mm jump rings before you begin building the chain.

Don't fret—
this bezel
is easy

Weave a chain mail bezel
with a built-in bail for a
rockin' guitar-pick pendant.

designed by John Wik

MATERIALS

pendant, 1½ x 1⅜ in. (3.8 x 3.5cm)

- brass jump rings:
  - **66** 20-gauge 3mm ID
  - **11** 18-gauge 4mm ID
- **11** black 18-gauge 4mm ID anodized-aluminum jump rings
- guitar picks
  - Fender 351 tortoiseshell, medium, standard
  - Fender 351 white, medium, standard
  - Dunlop stainless steel, thin, standard
- 32 in. (81.3cm) black leather cord, 1.8mm thick
- crimp-closure clasp (optional)
- **2** pairs of chainnose or flatnose pliers
- scrap wire, toothpick, or paper clip

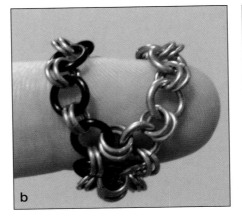

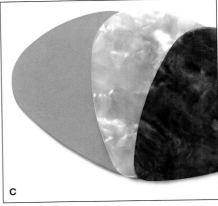

PROJECT NOTE:

A stainless steel pick adds some flash to the reverse side of the pendant.

► **1** Use two pairs of chainnose or flat-nose pliers to open 66 brass 3mm ID jump rings. Close 11 brass 4mm ID jump rings. Close 11 black anodized-aluminum 4mm ID jump rings.

► **2** Thread a 3mm brass jump ring through two 4mm brass jump rings, and close it. Repeat with a second 3mm brass ring. Separate the two 4mm rings so that they're on either side of the two 3mm rings, forming a 1+2+1 pattern.

► **3** Continue making this pattern until you've used all the 4mm brass rings and 22 of the 3mm rings. Connect the ends of the chain to make a loop.

► **4** Make another 1+2+1 chain, substituting the 4mm black rings for the 4mm brass rings. Connect the ends of the chain to make a loop [photo a].

► **5** Thread a 3mm ring through a 4mm brass ring in one chain loop and through a 4mm black ring in the other chain loop. Close the 3mm ring. Repeat with a second 3mm ring.

► **6** Continue to add seven more pairs of 3mm rings. On each chain loop, leave three consecutive 4mm

rings unconnected [photo b] so you can insert guitar picks later.

► **7** Arrange your three guitar picks as shown [photo c]. Make sure that any logos face inward and that the white pick is sandwiched between the other two.

NOTE: When you stack the picks on top of each other, placing the white pick in the middle brightens the translucent faux-tortoiseshell pick.

TIP: In guitar-pick lingo, "medium" refers to the thickness (gauge) of the pick. The term "standard" refers to the pick's shape. I chose the trio of picks for this project because they're all the same shape and their combined thickness is just right for the size of the jump rings I wanted to use to make the bezel.

► **8** Align the picks and insert them pointed-end first into the opening of the bezel [photo d]. (I inserted mine so that the side of the bezel with all brass rings would lie against the tortoiseshell pick.) It's okay if the rings are a little

PROJECT NOTE:

Guitar picks are as variable and distinctive as a classic guitar riff. Both a tool and an accessory, guitar picks are made in many colors, materials, and shapes. For example, faux versions of mother-of-pearl, tortoise-shell, and abalone are easy to find at local music shops and through online stores. You could easily swap the stainless steel pick and pair of plastic picks that are used in this project for something different — like picks that sport graphics, or collectible picks made of stone, wood, bone, or amber.

To create the pendant, you'll make a chain mail bezel to capture a stack of three guitar picks. The bezel also acts as a bail for the adjustable leather necklace cord. And because the pendant is reversible, it's really two necklaces in one. Once you've learned to weave a bezel of jump rings, you can use the same technique to enclose any other flat objects you'd like to display.

PROJECT NOTE:

It's always nice to have options. One way to add versatility to this necklace is to make the necklace cord adjustable by tying a pair of easy knots. Just follow this sequence of steps, and you'll be set to rock out in a choker or go for a more subdued look with a longer necklace.

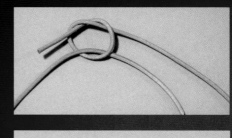

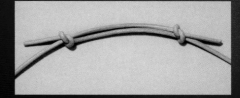

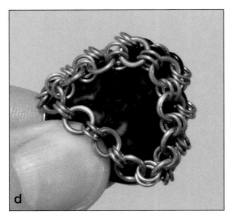

d

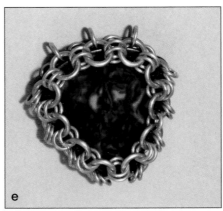

e

f

g

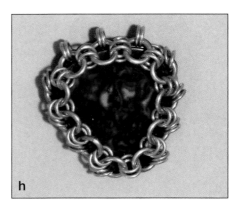

h

floppy; just make sure that the points of the picks are centered directly opposite the opening in the bezel.

► **9** The bezel's opening is made up of three pairs of unconnected 4mm jump rings. Thread one 3mm ring through the middle pair. Close the 3mm ring.

► **10** Although the bezel may feel a bit loose at this point, manipulate the jump rings so that they are aligned evenly around the guitar-pick sandwich. Make sure that the pointed ends of the picks line up across from the 3mm ring you just added.

► **11** Add one 3mm ring each to the remaining two pairs of unconnected 4mm jump rings **[photo e]**.

► **12** I use a bent piece of scrap wire to manipulate the jump rings so that the bezel creates a snug capture for the guitar picks **[photo f]**. You could also use a paper clip, toothpick, or other pointed tool — just take care not to

mar the surface of the guitar picks as you work.

► **13** After you've aligned the bezel to your liking, add another 3mm ring to each of the 4mm jump ring pairs at the short side of the assembly **[photo g]**.

► **14** Starting at the pointed end of the picks, thread a 32-in. (81cm) piece of 1.8mm-thick leather cord through the pairs of 3mm rings on the outside of the bezel. The pendant should look as shown **[photo h]**. You can add a crimp-closure clasp, or tie the ends of the cord to make an adjustable necklace (see Project Note).

Coils incognito

Coils of 14k gold-filled wire cleverly mimic jump rings in a fresh take on traditional chain mail.

designed by Leanne Soden

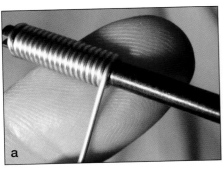

There's no shame in using gold-filled wire — it's more economical than solid gold and more durable than gold plate. Gold-filled wire (also called "rolled gold") is made from 100 times more gold than gold plate.

Making gold-filled wire involves bonding a sheet of 14k gold to a core of semiprecious metal, usually brass. Fabricating jewelry from gold-filled wire results in a beautiful piece at a fraction of the cost of 24k gold, and the wire lasts a lifetime; examples from the early 1900s still appear brand new.

Fortunately, the gold in this bracelet is affordable, even though your friends will think it cost you much more.

▶ **1** Hold a 3.5mm (⅛-in.) slotted steel mandrel in your nondominant hand. Place one end of a 9-ft. (2.7m) piece of gold-filled wire in the slot. Leave at least a ¼-in. (6mm) tail. Use your dominant hand to wind the wire toward you as you wrap it around the mandrel, making sure the wraps are tight and even **[photo a]**. Continue winding until the coil is 3 in. (7.6cm) long.

▶ **2** Slide the coil off the mandrel. Use super-flush or flush cutters to trim the tail close to the first wrap. Trim the wire on the opposite end of the coil close to the last wrap. Repeat to make a second coil the same length.

▶ **3** Hold a coil in your nondominant hand. Insert one jaw of your bentnose pliers between the second and third wrap, directly opposite the beginning of the wrap. Gently pull down on the longer part of the coil to create a small space between the first two complete rings and the rest of the coil **[photo b]**. Do not cut this set from the coil.

▶ **4** Repeat to create a small space between the fourth and fifth wraps and between the sixth and seventh wraps. Insert the pliers between the eighth and ninth wraps, but make a larger space **[photo c]** to accommodate wire cutters. Use wire cutters to cut the wire at the point where the fourth two-ring set ends **[photo d]**.

▶ **5** Use flatnose pliers to grasp a two-ring set at one end of the link,

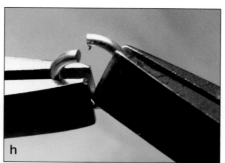

MATERIALS
bracelet, 7.5 in. (19.1cm)

- 9 ft. (2.7m) 20-gauge round dead-soft gold-filled wire
- sterling silver jump rings
  - **15** 16-gauge, 6mm ID
  - **28** 16-gauge, 4.5mm ID
  - **2** 16-gauge, 5.5mm ID
- medium sterling silver lobster claw clasp
- identification tag (optional)
- 3.5mm (⅛ in.) slotted steel mandrel
- super-flush or flush wire cutters
- bentnose pliers
- **2** pairs of flatnose pliers
- flat needle file
- soldering station (optional): torch, solder (easy), fire-resistant surface, (soldering pad, firebrick, charcoal block or steel tripod with fine steel screen), pickle pot with pickle, flux, anti-flux, steel tweezers (cross-locking and precision), copper tongs
- tumbler, steel shot, burnishing compound (optional)

making sure both rings are inside the jaws of the pliers. Do not squeeze the rings too tightly, or you could distort or scratch them. Use a second pair of flatnose pliers to grasp the adjacent two-ring set. Bend the first set at a 90-degree angle to the second one [photo e]. Repeat with each set. The end wires of the first and last sets should touch, but not overlap, in the center of the link. Use wire cutters to remove any excess [photo f]. The finished link should be symmetrical [photo g]. If the wire ends are rough, use a flat needle file to smooth them. Repeat to make a total of 15 X links.

▶ **6** You must work-harden your 6mm sterling silver jump rings (see Project Note on p. 84) before you use them. Hold a pair of flatnose pliers in each hand, and firmly grasp a 6mm jump ring on each side of the closure point. Move one half of the ring back and forth past the closure point [photo h]. Leave the jump ring wide open. Thread the jump ring through the center of all four sections of an X link [photo i]. Close the ring [photo j]. Repeat for the remaining X links.

▶ **7** Work-harden a 4.5mm ID jump ring, leaving it wide open. Thread the jump ring through one section of an X link. Repeat with a second X link [photo k]. Close the jump ring. Repeat on the opposite side of the two X links [photo l]. Repeat to connect the remaining links [photo m].

k

l

m

PROJECT NOTE:

When you strain metal past its yielding point, you work-harden it. While you are actually fatiguing the metal, the increased stress makes the metal stronger, which means it's less likely to distort later. The more you bend the metal, the harder it is to move.

In addition to bending, you can also stretch or hammer metal to harden it. Sterling silver and gold work-harden quickly; if you over-work them, they go from tough to brittle, and can break. Fine silver is softer than sterling, so it requires more work-hardening in order to make it resilient.

▶ **8** Work-harden a 5.5mm jump ring and slide a lobster claw clasp onto it. If you wish to attach an identification tag, do it now. On one end of the bracelet, open the end 6mm jump ring, and slide the 5.5mm jump ring onto it. Close the 6mm jump ring.

▶ **9** Attach a 5.5mm jump ring to the 6mm jump ring at the opposite end of the bracelet. You may solder the 5.5mm jump rings at each end of the bracelet closed, but work-hardening the jump rings is usually sufficient.

▶ **10** To make your bracelet shine, put it in a tumbler with steel shot and bur-nishing compound for 2–3 hours or until it has the desired finish.

splendor

Link five types of jump rings for a sinfully slinky chain mail necklace. This Persian-linked chain mail necklace is a chameleon of fine jewelry. Conservative enough to drape over a demure turtleneck dress for a business dinner, it will also go beautifully with velvet to an opera or make a smashing focal point above a plunging neckline for a night on the town.

designed by Julia Lowther

Process photos by Julia Lowther.

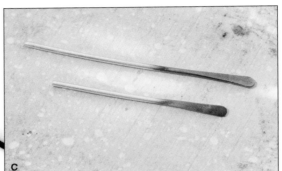

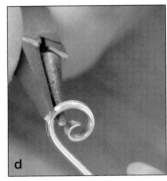

Hook-and-eye clasp

▶ **1** Cut two pieces of 16-gauge sterling silver wire, one 1½ in. (3.8cm), the other 2 in. (5cm). Make sure each wire is straight. The short piece will become the eye, and the long piece will become the hook. Forge a flat paddle shape on one end of each wire using a planishing hammer and a bench block or anvil [photo a]. Burs will form on the tips of each paddle.

▶ **2** Sand the burs smooth with 320- or 400-grit sandpaper [photo b]. Sand the short wire's unplanished end flat. Sand the long wire's unplanished end smooth and round. Since you have work-hardened the wires by forging them, they must be annealed [photo c] before forming.

TIP: Annealing is the process of heating work-hardened metal until it softens enough to be malleable. Put your metal on a fire-resistant surface, and heat the metal with a torch until it glows a subtle pink. Immediately remove the heat when you see the color, or you'll burn or melt the metal. Dim or turn off the lights to help you see this color change. To finish, quench the metal in water and put it in warm pickle to remove any oxides.

▶ **3** Using combination pliers (one flat jaw and one round jaw), roll the paddle of one wire into a curl, with the round jaw on the inside of the curl [photo d]. Roll until the flat section of the paddle touches the stem so that it can be soldered in place. Repeat with the other wire.

NOTE: If you use regular roundnose pliers, you will create small depressions on the outsides of the curls. You can space the depressions evenly around the outsides of the curls to convert a potential flaw into a pleasing design element. These "marks of process" are like fingerprints — they are unique to your piece and show that it was made by working hands rather than by a machine.

▶ **4** Flux the long wire, and place it on a fire-resistant surface. Place a small pallion of easy solder where the curl touches the stem. Heat the piece until the solder flows. Quench it in water, place it in warm pickle, and rinse it. Make sure the join is secure [photo e].

▶ **5** Gently planish the rounded end of the long wire into a small paddle shape without thinning it too much. Grasp this paddle with your

combination pliers with the round jaw on the same side as the curl. Bend the paddle toward the curl at an 85-degree angle [photo f]. Grasp the stem halfway between the paddle and the curl with the flat jaw of your combination pliers on the same side of the wire as the curl. Gently shape the wire into a hook [photo g]. Planish the curved top of the hook [photo h]. This will work-harden the hook so that it will hold the eye firmly.

▶ **6** Make a simple loop using the straight end of the short wire. Adjust this loop to make the eye look like a figure 8 [photo i].

▶ **7** Solder the eye. Flux the eye, and place it on a fire-resistant surface. Place small pallions of easy solder where the curl and the end of the simple loop touch the wire stem. Heat the piece until the solder flows. Quench, pickle, and rinse it. Make sure the joins are secure [photo j].

▶ **8** Use your pliers to rotate the eye's simple loop 90 degrees so it lies perpendicular to the curl. Test the hook and the eye to make sure they are a good fit. Gently open or close the hook with your combination pliers to correct the fit.

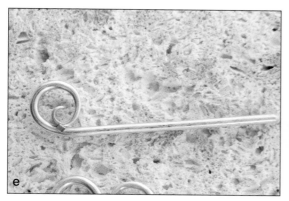

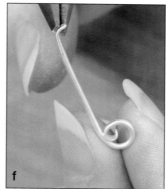

► **9** Work-harden and restore the shine to your newly finished clasp by tumbling the pieces.

Tapered chain

You will need the following jump rings: Either make them by following steps 1–2 below, or purchase them from a jewelry-making supplier.

- **40** 14-gauge, 8.7mm ID (¹¹⁄₃₂-in. mandrel)
- **56** 16-gauge, 6.7mm ID (¹⁷⁄₆₄-in. mandrel)
- **64** 18-gauge, 5.5mm ID (⁷⁄₃₂-in. mandrel)
- **88** 20-gauge, 4.4mm ID (¹¹⁄₆₄-in. mandrel)
- **120** 22-gauge, 3.6mm ID (⁹⁄₆₄-in. mandrel)

► **1** Wind wire and cut jump rings (optional). Use a set of transfer punches as mandrels to make creating jump rings easy. The intended use of transfer punches is to exactly transfer the location of a hole from one sheet of metal to another. They usually come in sets of 28 or more and consist of perfectly round steel rods of different diameters. Other cylindrical items make acceptable mandrels as long as they have diameters to match the jump ring diameters needed.

► **2** Place the mandrel in the chuck of a hand drill, cordless drill, or winder. Secure the end of your wire between two of the chuck jaws, and bend the wire perpendicular to the mandrel. Begin winding with one hand (or turn the drill on a slow speed) while holding the wire with the other to make an

MATERIALS

necklace, 18 in. (46cm)

- sterling silver wire
  - 14-gauge round, half-hard, 1.2 troy oz. (or 40 rings, 8.7mm ID)
  - 16-gauge round, half-hard, 0.80 troy oz. (or 56 rings, 6.7mm ID)
  - 16-gauge round, half-hard, 4 in. (10.2cm)
  - 18-gauge round, half-hard, 0.50 troy oz. (or 64 rings, 5.5mm ID)
  - 20-gauge round, half-hard, 0.35 troy oz. (or 88 rings, 4.4mm ID)
  - 22-gauge round, half-hard, 0.30 troy oz. (or 120 rings, 3.6mm ID)
- side cutters
- steel bench block or anvil
- planishing hammer
- sanding stick, 320 or 400 grit
- soldering station: torch, easy solder, fire-resistant surface (soldering pad, firebrick, or charcoal block), pickle pot with pickle, flux, steel tweezers (cross locking and precision), copper tongs
- combination (one round jaw and one flat jaw) chainnose and flatnose, or 2 pairs parallel jaw
- tumbler with fine-porcelain tumbling media and burnishing liquid
- scrap silver (optional)
- liver of sulfur (optional)
- transfer punch set or mandrels of appropriate diameters (optional)
- hand drill, cordless drill, or winder (optional)
- jeweler's saw, 2/0 blades (optional)
- 6 in. (15cm) 24–26 gauge copper wire or wire from a twist tie, or needle

Materials note:

If you are buying premade jump rings and the supplier does not carry the exact inside diameter needed, choose the closest diameter that is a bit larger than the diameter called for.

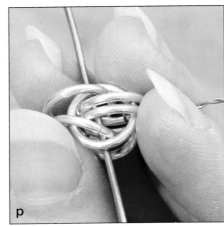

even spring with no gaps between the winds [photo k].

► **3** Use a jeweler's saw with a 2/0 blade to cut lengthwise down the spring either on or off the mandrel [photo l]. The best angle for the saw is one that results in the blade cutting into three rings at a time. Repeat these steps with mandrels of different diameters and wire of different gauges to make all the jump rings needed.

► **4** Begin by building the large midsection of the chain using 14-gauge jump rings. Close two 14-gauge rings using chainnose and flatnose pliers or two pairs of parallel-jaw pliers. Link two 14-gauge rings through the two closed rings, and close this second pair. Link two 14-gauge rings through the last two rings added, and close this third pair [photo m].

► **5** Attach a thin wire handle (24- to 26-gauge copper, or wire from a twist tie) to the four rings on one end [photo n]. Hold the wire handle in your nondominant hand and your pliers in your dominant hand. Position the third pair of rings to the outsides of the first pair, creating a V [photo o].

► **6** This next step is all-important! Cut a 3-in. (7.6cm) piece of thin wire to use as a guide. Or, use a needle for a sturdier guide. Slide your guide into the rings from the side: go between the second pair of rings, through the right third of the third pair of rings, and through the left third of the first pair of rings [photo p].

► **7** Follow the path of the guide with two open 14-gauge rings, one at a time. Close the rings away from the wire handle [photo q].

► **8** Attach two 14-gauge rings to the last pair added, and close them. Position the new rings to the outsides of the previous V created [photo r]. Slide your guide in place through the new tier as in step 6.

► **9** Repeat steps 7–8, placing your guide through the new tier each time, until all the 14-gauge rings are used [photo s].

► **10** With the rest of the jump rings, alternate between building one end of the chain and the other. Attach half of the rings of each size to one end and the other half to the other end. Taper the necklace back to the clasp by

assembling the rings in order of decreasing size. Repeating the pattern from steps 6–8 on each side, add:

- **28** 16-gauge rings
- **32** 18-gauge rings
- **44** 20-gauge rings
- **60** 22-gauge rings

► **11** Add or remove 22-gauge jump rings evenly on both ends of the necklace until you reach the proper length.

► **12** Gently open one of the last four rings on one end of the necklace. Slip the curl end of the hook through the ring, and close the ring. Repeat with the remaining three of the last four rings. When you are finished, the hook should be attached to the necklace by all four of the last rings on one end [photo t]. Repeat on the other end of the necklace to attach the eye.

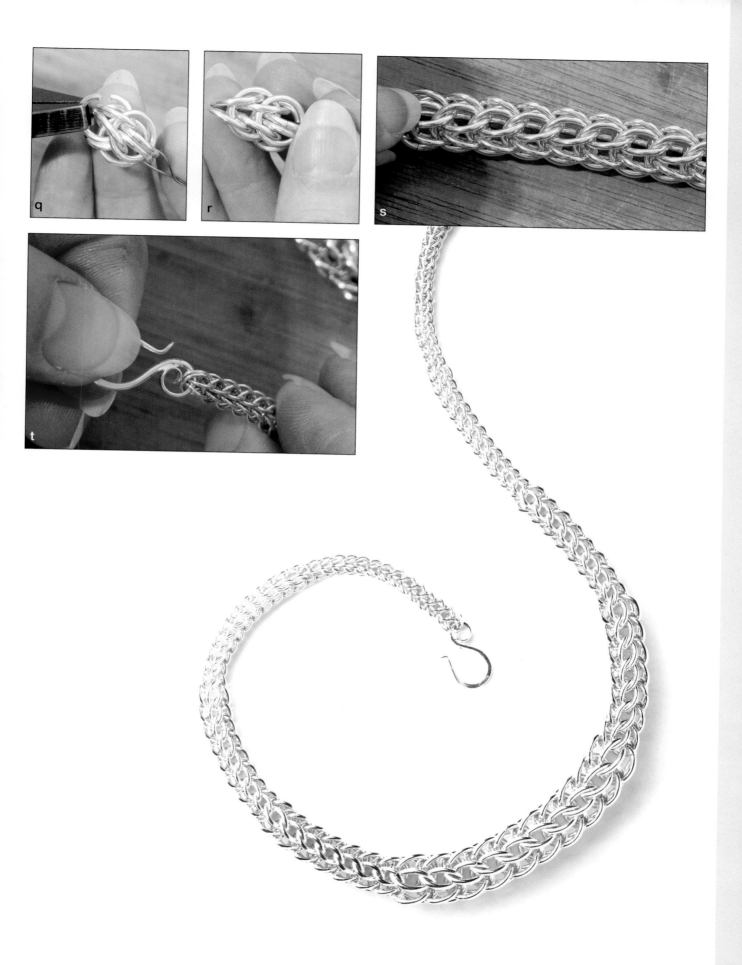

time-honored
Heracles knot

designed by Howard Siegel

This modern necklace marries two traditional chain-making motifs: the Heracles knot's shaped and interlocking rings, and the Byzantine chain pattern. The Heracles knot, with its interlinked halves, is a centuries-old visual motif symbolizing marriage, so it's use is fitting in this necklace, which marries two distinct traditional chain patterns. You'll use basic fusing and shaping to create the Heracles knots, then make Byzantine chain segments to connect them. These simple, easily mastered techniques result in an elegant chain.

MATERIALS

necklace, 16 in. (41cm)
- approximately 50 18-gauge fine-silver jump rings, 12mm ID
- sterling silver jump rings
  - **200** 20-gauge, 3mm ID
  - **2** 16-gauge, 4–5mm ID
- 13mm lobster claw clasp
- roundnose pliers
- Optivisor or other magnifier
- mandrels, 7mm (9/32 in.) and 3mm (1/8 in.)
- bench vise
- skewer
- paste solder: easy or extra easy

Supply note:
- 2 pairs of chainnose or flatnose pliers
- soldering station: torch, solder (easy), fire-resistant surface, (soldering pad, firebrick, charcoal block or steel tripod with fine steel screen), pickle pot with pickle, flux, anti-flux, steel tweezers (cross-locking and precision), copper tongs

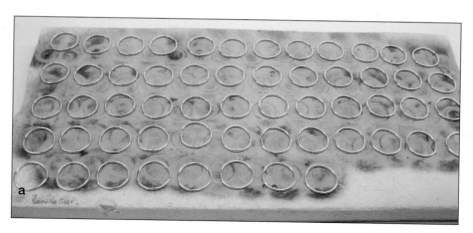

Heracles knots
Rings

▶ **1** Fusing is a technique in which you heat metal (in this case, the cut ends of a jump ring) almost to its melting point in order to join it without using solder. Fine silver responds especially well to fusing.

▶ **2** To properly fuse your jump rings, their cut ends must be aligned flush. Use either a pair of chainnose pliers and your fingers or two pairs of pliers to grasp a jump ring. Slightly over-form the ring by bringing the ends of the ring past each other, then together so they touch and align.

▶ **3** Check the alignment of the join by looking at the closed ring from the edge and from above. Repeat to tightly close approximately 50 fine-silver rings.

NOTE: The cut ends of the rings must be in complete contact in order for the joins to fuse.

▶ **4** Place the closed rings in rows on a soldering pad so that the join of each ring faces the front of the pad [photo a]. Placing the rings so that each join is in the same relative position

makes it easier to find and watch the joins during fusing.

▶ **5** Place the soldering pad on a firebrick; this raises the pad above the surface of your bench, minimizing the possibility of burning your benchtop. At this point, put on your Optivisor; its magnification helps you see the tiny joins more clearly.

TIP: When you're fusing, dim the room lights. Each ring will turn red and "flash" when its join fuses; you'll be able to see these changes better in a dark room.

▶ **6** Light the torch and adjust the flame to about half of the flame length available. Starting with the jump ring at the left rear of the soldering pad, move the tip of the flame in a circular motion over the ring, following the jump ring's shape.

▶ **7** When the ring becomes dull red, move the flame tip to the ring's join, and move the flame in a tight circular motion, uniformly heating both sides of the join **[photo b]**. Watch for the metal at the join to flow; when the metal flows, its surface becomes more reflective. This is called the "flash."

NOTE: When you see the flash, immediately remove the flame. Overheating will result in thinning the ring at the join or completely burning through the ring.

▶ **8** Fuse all the rings, moving from left to right along the last row of rings, then from right to left along the next row forward.

▶ **9** Secure a ⁹/₃₂-in. (7mm) mandrel horizontally in a bench vise. Slide a fused fine-silver ring onto the mandrel. Pull the ring up against the bottom of the mandrel so that there's space in the ring above the mandrel.

▶ **10** Place a ⅛-in. (3mm) mandrel through the ring above the ⁹/₃₂-in. (7mm) mandrel. Pull up gently with the ⅛-in. (3mm) mandrel to elongate the ring.

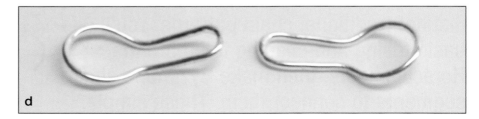

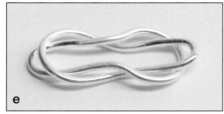

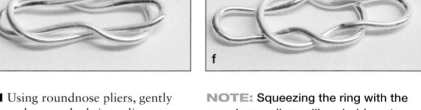

▶ **11** Using roundnose pliers, gently squeeze the stretched ring adjacent to the ⁹/₃₂-in. mandrel **[photo c]** and then adjacent to the ⅛-in. mandrel. The objective is to form each ring so that the finished shape resembles a keyhole. The elongated sides of the ring should be parallel.

NOTE: Squeezing the ring with the roundnose pliers will probably not result in a perfectly shaped keyhole; run the ⅛-in. mandrel along the elongated sides of the ring to make them parallel.

▶ **12** Form all the fine-silver rings into the keyhole shape.

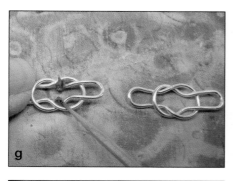

g

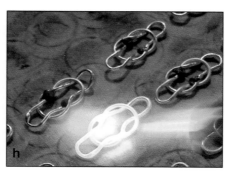

h

i

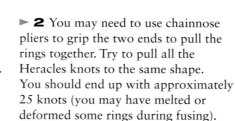

j

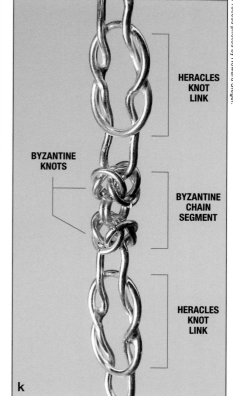

k

Process photos by Howard Siegel.

HERACLES KNOT LINK

BYZANTINE KNOTS

BYZANTINE CHAIN SEGMENT

HERACLES KNOT LINK

▶ **13** Using chainnose pliers, grasp across the circular part of a keyhole-shaped ring. Using your fingers, bend the elongated end up about 20 degrees. Repeat to form all the keyhole rings.

Knot assembly

▶ **1** Position two of the keyhole rings so that the elongated ends face each other [photo d]. Slide each elongated end into the opposite circular opening [photo e], pulling the ends until the keyhole rings nest snugly [photo f]. Slightly bend each elongated end to hold the rings in place.

▶ **2** You may need to use chainnose pliers to grip the two ends to pull the rings together. Try to pull all the Heracles knots to the same shape. You should end up with approximately 25 knots (you may have melted or deformed some rings during fusing).

▶ **3** Place the assembled knots on the soldering pad in rows. For each knot, use a skewer to place a small amount (about the size of two pinheads) of easy or extra easy paste solder on the inside of the knot at the two points where the wires cross [photo g].

▶ **4** Use your torch to heat each knot until the paste solder flows on each join [photo h].

▶ **5** Pickle the soldered knots, rinse them in running water, and blot them dry with a paper towel.

Byzantine chain

▶ **1** Open 200 20-gauge 0.8mm sterling silver jump rings.

▶ **2** Place a twist tie or paper clip through one end of a Heracles knot. Slide a jump ring through the other end of the knot, and close the ring. Repeat with a second jump ring.

▶ **3** Slide a jump ring through both of the jump rings you just added, and close it. Repeat with a second jump ring. The configuration should now be two jump rings through two jump rings, which are through one end of a Heracles knot.

▶ **4** Separate the second pair of rings so that one ring falls to each side. Place an awl through the first pair of rings, and allow the second pair of rings to fall so that they lie next to the Heracles knot [photo i] on each side.

▶ **5** Grasping the Heracles knot and the two rings beside it, remove the awl. Push the second two jump rings up inside the first two rings.

▶ **6** Use the awl to separate the first two rings, exposing the upper curve of the second two rings. Insert the awl through the second pair of rings, causing the rings to move into the proper position.

NOTE: Do not put the awl through the Heracles knot. The awl should be above the knot.

▶ **7** Remove the awl. Grasp the flat side of the Heracles knot and the jump rings with your thumb and forefinger to hold the rings in place with an opening between the "V" formed by two of the rings. (This was the space occupied by the awl.)

▶ **8** Slide a jump ring through the opening in the V formed by the first four rings [photo j]. Close this ring just enough that it cannot come loose; do not close it completely. You have formed a Byzantine knot.

▶ **9** Add two pairs of jump rings to one end of a second Heracles knot. Form a Byzantine knot as before. Slide a jump ring through the V in the knot. While this ring is still open, slide it through the V in the Byzantine knot that you formed on the previous Heracles knot. Close the ring. Open the partially closed ring in the center of the first Byzantine knot, insert it through the V in the second Byzantine knot, and close the ring.

NOTE: At this point, you should have a symmetrical Byzantine chain segment between two Heracles knot links; a Byzantine knot should be adjacent to each Heracles knot and two jump rings should connect the Byzantine knots.

▶ **10** Continue connecting the Heracles knot links with Byzantine chain segments until the chain reaches the desired length [photo k].

Assembly and finishing

▶ **1** Remove the twist tie or paper clip from the starter Heracles knot. Slide a 16-gauge jump ring through the end Heracles knot, and slide a lobster claw clasp onto the jump ring. Close the jump ring. The clasp can hook through the last Heracles knot on the other end of the chain. Or, if needed, add another 16-gauge jump ring to this end of the chain to properly orient the clasp.

▶ **2** Place the assembled chain into a tumbler, and tumble the chain for about an hour. Tumbling will polish and harden the chain, as well as remove any burs that resulted when the jump rings were cut. Check to make sure that there are no remaining burs; if there are, tumble again for as long as needed to remove the burs. Additional tumbling will not damage the chain.

PROJECT NOTE:
If you have any surplus Heracles knots, you can make matching earrings simply by adding ear wires.

Contributors

PENNEY ACOSTA received a degree in fine arts 35 years ago, but now works fulltime in an unrelated field. Her jewelry work uses many different media, but she says her imagination is still in its infancy. Contact Penney via e-mail at penneya2@aol.com.

Contact **PHYLLIS ADAMS** in care of Kalmbach Books.

Traveling around the country including 13 years in Alaska provided **SANDY AMAZEEN** with plenty of exposure to different cultures and artistic possibilities. She now resides in Williams, AZ busily teaching, hiking, rock hounding, wire wrapping, doing lapidary work and creating wearable art. Contact Sandy via e-mail at amamess@earthlink.net.

KIMBERLY BERLIN has been creating wire art for many years and she loves to incorporate wire into her beading projects. Currently, she is teaching wire art classes in San Antonio, Texas. Contact Kimberly via e-mail at berlik@flash.net.

LUAN CARNEVALE is the owner of Life's A Bead in Belmont, MA. She devotes all of her time to beading, wire work, chain maille and more! Luan can be contacted at lifesabead@comcast.net or through her store at www.lifesabead.com.

MIACHELLE DEPIANO is a technical writer for both a major computer corporation and a publishing company She makes jewelry specializing in wire sculpture and chain maille, and dabbles in photography as well. Contact Miachelle via e-mail at mdepiano@coxnet.

JOHN FETVEDT finds chain making interesting because it combines art, mathematics, and construction techniques into each different chain pattern. He can be contacted at fetvedt@mindspring.com or through his website, www.bijoux-de-terre.com.

AMANDA SHERO GRANSTROM lives in Portland, Ore. She loves color, whether working with beads, fibers, polymer clay, glass, or chain mail. Amanda has been designing and crafting jewelry since 2001. Contact her via e-mail at amanda@redeftshibori.com, or visit her website, craftycatjumprings.com.

WENDY HUNT is a jewelry designer who lives in Ontario, Canada. She began designing chain mail and beaded jewelry since 2004. To see more of Wendy's designs, visit her website, baublesnbeads.atspace.com, or contact her via e-mail at hunt7897@rogers.com

DEANNA KITTRELL has been beading for years, and chain mail is one of her favorite techniques. She works at Piece of Mind, a bead store where she gets inspiration from the owner Gretchen Schueller. Contact her via e-mail at dsdesigns@surewest.net, or visit her website, dsdesignsjewelry.com.

Contact **MARIE CRISTINE KNUFF** in care of Kalmbach Books.

Contact **ESTHER LEE** in care of Kalmbach Books.

JULIE LOWTHER lives in Seattle and writes articles and teaches classes on chain making. Her work is showcased in numerous books and magazines. Visit her website, julialowther.com.

SUSAN MATYCH-HAGER, Professor Emerita of Music at Siena Heights University in Adrian, Mich., is a full-time lampworker and jewelry designer. She and her jewelry-design partner, **KATHY PETERSEN**, were included in the 2009 Convergence juried collaboration exhibit cospon-sored by the International Society of Glass Beadmakers and Bead&Button magazine. Contact her via e-mail at susan@hagerstudiosglass.com, or visit her website, hagerstudiosglass.com.

Contact **ANNE MITCHELL** via e-mail at anne@annemitchell.net, or visit her website, annemitchell.net.

KATHY PETERSEN is a retired school psychologist and hobbyist jewelry fabricator. She is skilled in metalwork, lapidary, wire weaving, and chain mail. She teaches chain mail and jewelry-making classes at the Gem and Rockhound Club in Toledo, Ohio, and at Bonita Bead Boutique in Maumee, Ohio. Contact her via e-mail at kpetersendesigns@aol.com.

HOWARD SIEGEL'S chain-making articles have been published in magazines and books, and his recent chain designs incorporate pearls, beads, and corrugation. For more information, visit laptiqueltd.bravehost.com.

LEANNE SODEN designs jewelry that embraces centuries-old chain-making techniques. Contact her in care of Kalmbach Books.

Contact **DEBORAH THOMPSON** in care of Kalmbach Books.

HAZEL WHEATON is the Editor of *Art Jewelry* magazine. Contact her at hwheaton@kalmbach.com.

JOHN WIK is an artist and jeweler from Minnesota who enjoys incorporating commonly found items into his work. He can be contacted via email at artistreason@gmail.com.